"*The Sacredness of Secular Work* does an extraordinary job of being both personally relevant and, more importantly, biblically faithful. It's well written with excellent illustrations. It's not often I read a book that deals with heaven, the new earth, or eternal reward where I feel like the author really gets it. Jordan Raynor has done his homework and really gets it. I think the smile of God is on this book, and I'm happy to recommend it."

—RANDY ALCORN, *New York Times* bestselling author of *Heaven, The Promise of the New Earth,* and *The Law of Rewards*

"*The Sacredness of Secular Work* is theologically rich *and* terrifically practical. If you've ever felt like a second-class Christian because you're not a pastor or 'full-time missionary,' this book is about to change your life."

—MARK BATTERSON, *New York Times* bestselling author of *The Circle Maker* and pastor at National Community Church

"For the believer, there is no such thing as a second-class secular job. Whether you lead a Christian organization or run a real-estate business, the way you work counts for all of eternity. How you conduct yourself in the workplace reveals, as nothing else will, the real you. And the way you do your work influences everyone up and down the office hallways. My friend Jordan Raynor explores this and other themes in *The Sacredness of Secular Work*. So, if you want to be a good steward of Christ's gospel in the world's marketplace, you hold in your hands the best of guides!"

—JONI EARECKSON TADA, founder of Joni and
Friends International Disability Center

"This book is a paradigm-shifting, face-punching, grace-filled manifesto on what it means to be a working, creating Christian in our modern age. It's a manual to take with you, dog-eared and aged, as a reminder that your work isn't just work; your work is holy, no matter how small or mundane. By the end, you will look at every part of your work, from keyboard strokes to diaper changes, Zoom calls to dirty dishes, as a chance to tear open the veil and yank more of the kingdom of heaven into our world now."

—LUKE LEFEVRE, founder of Holy Work

"Our work needs a new story—a true and timeless story that embraces the intrinsic value of our work and sees our daily labors through the meaningful vantage point of an eternal horizon. With theological acumen, unusual clarity, and practical wisdom, Jordan Raynor skillfully brushes away the dense overgrowth of an all-too-prevalent impoverished theology of work. I highly recommend this book!"

—TOM NELSON, lead pastor of Christ Community Church
and author of *Work Matters*

"When people ask why I left full-time ministry, I tell them I never left. The idea that full-time ministry is reserved for a pastor or missionary is theologically incorrect. For too long now, the work of Jesus followers in the marketplace has often been portrayed as less than, or not as important as, those in traditional ministry roles. It's one of the many reasons why I believe Jordan's new book is both needed and an important wake-up call for us all. If you follow Jesus and go to work, congratulations. You're in full-time ministry."

—JEFF HENDERSON, bestselling author of *What To Do Next*

"Do. Not. Read. Jordan Raynor's gonna mess with your neatly compartmentalized life, throw your theological constructs about faith and work into disarray, and convince you that your work matters to God. You might actually start integrating your faith into your daily tasks. The next thing you know, you'll make your life messy by blurring the lines between the sacred and the mundane. Engage your spirit and soul at work? Believe that God rewards us for doing our jobs in ways that glorify him, benefit others, and bring God's kingdom to earth? Bah humbug. Enjoy the bliss of keeping work in its secular box, separate from your faith. It's safer. Simpler. Even if it is bad theology."

—ROY TINKLENBERG, founder, CEO, and city catalyst at Faith and Work Movement Global

"*The Sacredness of Secular Work* is as prophetic as it is practical, re-enchanting us to see the work of our hands as worship and of eternal worth. This book is for the poet, the pastor, the pharmacist, and the plumber. It's for the jaded and the disenchanted, those pining to live with purpose. With wit and wisdom, Raynor will revolutionize the ways in which you see your place in the world. Deeply insightful, irrevocably instrumental . . . I dare you to let this book rekindle passion, delighting you to see and believe that your labor for the Lord is not in vain."

—RACHEL MARIE KANG, author of *Let There Be Art* and *The Matter of Little Losses*

"I have been laboring at the elimination of the misunderstanding of the sacred-secular duality for over four decades. We've made a lot of progress, but the problem persists perniciously. Jordan Raynor makes an energetic, logical, and compelling argument for a renewed understanding of a much bigger gospel and a much bigger vision for vocation. Open up this book, and open up a much bigger invitation to participate in God's adventure in the world."

—DAVE EVANS, coauthor of *Designing Your Life,* cofounder of the Stanford Life Design Lab, and venture partner at Praxis Labs

"It's easy to believe that you have to work in a nonprofit or the church for your work to matter. But this simply isn't true. Jordan teaches believers how to reclaim the authority, purpose, and significance that they already have in the work they're already doing. His book will show you that there's no difference between ministry and marketplace. When God is in you, it's all ministry! And that is good news for all of us."

—CHRISTY WRIGHT, author of *Business Boutique* and *Take Back Your Time* and former Ramsey Personality

"If every Christian were to view their work as a calling from God, we would see a radical transformation in the way that the church engages with the world. This book has the power to accelerate that transformation. Theologically deep and easy to read, *The Sacredness of Secular Work* is about to become one of the most highlighted books on your shelf."

—PAUL SOHN, director of the Center for Faith & Work at Redeemer Presbyterian Church and author of *Quarter-Life Calling*

"Jordan Raynor has written a book that allows every reader to see the impact of serving Christ right where they work. The light we carry is like a beacon in the world. Living for Him is sharing the gospel through the life we live around those we work with. This book will inspire you to keep your lamp trimmed and be ready to answer the call every day you work."

—ANNE BEILER, founder of Auntie Anne's Pretzels, author, and speaker

"It's difficult to express my wild enthusiasm for *The Sacredness of Secular Work*. Jordan is a voice for the next generation of faith-and-work thinkers and workers. He has an amazing gift of conveying deep theological truths with humor and everyday relevance. You will never view your job and church the same. This is a fantastic and inspiring read."

—DAVE HATAJ, author of *Good Work* and owner of Edgerton Gear

"Without downplaying the importance of evangelism, Raynor's theologically accessible and delightfully practical book lifts up our 'first commission' work of culture-making and imaginatively connects it to our eternal labors. His responses to the question of whether our work truly matters for eternity gave me new food for thought. The book will strengthen believers' confidence that God sees and delights in their ordinary work done with other-centeredness and excellence."

—DR. AMY L. SHERMAN, author of *Kingdom Calling* and *Agents of Flourishing*

"Jordan has done something of the impossible. *The Sacredness of Secular Work* brings together a host of sources and adeptly goes after lingering half-truths with sharp wit and disarming insight. This new offering is a thoroughly researched, deeply engaging, and dare I say needed addition to the conversation on faith and work. I couldn't put it down!"

—ANDREW NEMR, TED fellow, international tap dance artist, educator, and speaker

"I absolutely love this book! Jordan helps believers remember that they are called to a throne as kings and queens redeemed by Christ to rule and reign over every square inch of their industries with God and for him. If you want to feel fully alive in your current work, read *The Sacredness of Secular Work* now!"

—MICHAEL ARRIETA, CEO of Garden City Equity

"*The Sacredness of Secular Work* should be required reading for all Christians."

—MATT RUSTEN, president of Made to Flourish

"Jordan's book is like putting on a pair of glasses for the first time and seeing how, no matter your vocation, the work you do in this world for His sake has eternal significance. You're living a grander story than you ever realized, and Jordan shows how your role is divinely purposed."

—JOSHUA STRAUB, PhD, author of *Famous at Home*

"Believers desperately need to grasp why and how their work is already missionary activity rather than just an occasion for it. Jordan Raynor will help you grasp those truths in this theologically sound yet terrifically accessible book!"

—DR. DARRELL COSDEN, author of *The Heavenly Good of Earthly Work* and former professor of theological studies at Judson University

"Jordan takes on some huge, critical, and timely questions in this book. As leaders navigating a fast-changing world, it is crucial we do not grab for the next program or project innovation before doing deep reflection on foundational beliefs. I welcome Jordan's curiosity and admire his courage, and have benefited from the insights he brings in this book."

—ANDREW SCOTT, CEO of Operation Mobilization USA

"As a homeschool mom to four sons who has made the Great Commission a central family focus, I was thrilled to find that *The Sacredness of Secular Work* does not minimize the importance of sharing the gospel. Instead, it magnifies the totality of the work we do as Christ followers: From dish washing to data analytics, professional surfing to proofreading, doing excellent work for God's glory is a high and holy calling. My sons will all be getting a copy of this book!"

—MONICA SWANSON, author of *Raising Amazing* and host of the *Monica Swanson Podcast*

"Jordan invites us into a greater story, adventure, and understanding of the full gospel. If the whole church (including *you*) lived the whole gospel to the whole world (including in your daily work), what a world it would be! I'm grateful for this book."

—MIKE SHARROW, CEO of C12 Business Forums

"Jordan hits on an important theme: The Great Commission is not the only commission Jesus left us. The kingdom of God is much bigger than that. And that truth has profound implications for seeing the sacredness of your seemingly 'secular' work. I am honored and happy to endorse this great book!"

—DR. ROSS O'BRIEN, director of the Graduate School of Business at Dallas Baptist University

"From his years of work in the tech sector, Jordan has an incredible understanding that a Christ follower makes an eternal difference in others' lives not just by what they say but also by how they work! As a pastor, I pray that my people who work in offices, boardrooms, and locker rooms during the week will see that God has a plan for the spaces and places where He has put them! This book will become a textbook for this transformation!"

—MIKE LINCH, senior pastor of NorthStar Church

"Dismantling the line between the secular and the sacred, Jordan Raynor invites us to live as if on a mission, even if we are not career missionaries. We do not need to work in vocational ministries to see ministry opportunities all around us in our various vocations. Goodness, if we all worked within the church, how would the church get out into the world?! This is one of the most important conversations we need to have in Christendom today."

—WENDY SPEAKE, author of *The 40-Day Sugar Fast* and *The 40-Day Feast*

"In typical Jordan Raynor style, this book is easy to read but gives you a lot to think about. If you labor at all—paid or unpaid, in the ministry, the home, or the marketplace—it's worth your time to wrestle through the meaning of your work. Through Scripture and stories, Jordan offers ideas and guidance for those looking to do that well."

—SARAH EEKHOFF ZYLSTRA, senior writer and editor at the Gospel Coalition

"Jordan unpacks the dignity and meaning that work provides us and shows how all work allows us to experience God. He destroys the myth of the secular-sacred delineations of work and clearly articulates the liberating truth that all work is an act of worship. If you would like to embark on an adventure to find significant meaning and true joy in your work, this book is a must-read."

—LARRY GRIFFITH, CEO of Corporate Chaplains of America

"This book is such a refreshing shift in our thinking about how much value our day-to-day work has for the kingdom of God, showing us that the impact of our work can be immeasurably more than we could ever imagine."

—ANITA CORSINI, cofounder of Red Barn Homes and HGTV star

"I believe in this work so much. This book is what the world needs right now as leaders take their place not only in the pulpit but also wherever they find their vocations."

—MIGNON FRANCOIS, founder of the Cupcake Collection

"I believe the workplace is our most important mission field. *The Sacredness of Secular Work* makes a compelling case for the need for all of us to be bi-vocational; focused equally on both our ministry and career."

—SEAN KOUPLEN, chairman and CEO of Regent Bank and author of *94X*

"The way we talk about our lives and our work can dramatically change the way we live and work. In that light, the line many have drawn between 'sacred' and 'secular' has caused stress for many women and men who were truly called to work outside the lines of institutional religion. What Jordan has done with this book is provide a way to reframe our relationship with the work God calls us to, regardless of the specifics of the job."

—JUSTIN MCROBERTS, author of *Sacred Strides*

"Jordan's unique perspective, with hands in both the business and ministry worlds, infuses his words with genuine authenticity. This isn't just theory; it's his firsthand testimony of God's faithfulness. If you're ready to break down the walls between the secular and the sacred in your life and work, this book will encourage and equip you to do so."

—MICHELLE MYERS, cohost of the *She Works His Way* podcast, author, and speaker

"What does it mean to do the 'work' of God? Jordan Raynor approaches this topic with passion and deep insight. He breaks our religious icons, offering new ways of thinking about daily work, sharing faith, and God's biggest purposes for us. He introduces a 'purpose-driven life' that takes us beyond what we might have thought. You may not buy all of his passionate statements, but you should hear and weigh them!"

—ALBERT ERISMAN, retired Boeing executive, board chairman for the Theology of Work Project, and author of *The Accidental Executive* and *Living with Purpose in a Polarizing World*

"One of the greatest gifts in my life has been learning to approach my vocation as a baker as an act of prayer. In *The Sacredness of Secular Work*, Jordan Raynor shows how every job contributes to God's work in the world. Whether you labor with your hands, at a desk, or in front of a classroom, this book will help you understand more fully the eternal value of your daily rhythms."

—KENDALL VANDERSLICE, author of *By Bread Alone*

"People of God who see their vocational lives as an act of worship and worthy of intentionality will change the trajectory of the Christian church in our generation. You will be challenged and blessed as you read this very important book."

—DANIEL FUSCO, pastor, author, TV and radio host

"This book will encourage you to embrace how your work truly matters for eternity. Jordan provides a timely and practical perspective on the sacredness of your work."

—BRAD LOMENICK, founder of BLINC and author of
H3 Leadership and *The Catalyst Leader*

"You don't have to be on your church's staff to do ministry. If you take care of your kids or your neighbor, you are doing ministry. If you put great products and services out into the world that truly help people, you are doing ministry. But that can be so hard to see, given the language we use in the church. Jordan is your guide to a better way. In this book, you will find the freedom you've been looking for to embrace your work as your primary ministry in the world."

—GRAHAM COCHRANE, TEDx speaker and author of
How to Get Paid for What You Know

"The world desperately needs to see a display of what God is like. But many Christians feel guilty for working in the very places where that display is most needed. This theologically sound and supremely practical book will free you from that guilt and convince you that your 'secular' work is very sacred indeed!"

—DR. ANDREAS KÖSTENBERGER, cofounder of Biblical
Foundations and theologian in residence at Fellowship Raleigh

"This is a profoundly helpful and important book. Every Christian is 'first-rate,' and secular vocations are not only permissible but valuable. Don't believe me? Read this book!"

—MATT PERMAN, author of *What's Best Next*

"Jordan Raynor has, with great wisdom and biblical insight, spoken truth that every Christian in the workforce needs to hear. *The Sacredness of Secular Work* is an amazing and life-changing book. Read this book, and give a copy to all your friends."

—DR. STEVE BROWN, professor at Reformed Theological Seminary and podcast host at Key Life ministries

"Jordan understands the crucial need to get past the old 'Great Commission only' definition of faith and work. Through personal stories, practical insights, and biblical wisdom, his book will challenge readers with the idea that secular work matters for eternity!"

—DAVID ROTH, founder of Workmatters

"Have you ever struggled with seeing worth, purpose, or value in your work because you are not in 'full-time ministry?' Jordan will take you on a journey to see God's eternal purposes and intrinsic worth in your work right now, and how your work can contribute to eternity, bringing you joy and God glory."

—CHRIS BASHAM, lead pastor at the Church at Odessa

The Sacredness of Secular Work

The Sacredness of Secular Work

4 Ways Your Job
Matters for Eternity
(Even When You're Not
Sharing the Gospel)

Jordan Raynor

WATERBROOK

Published in the United States by WaterBrook, an imprint of Random House, a division of Penguin Random House LLC.

WATERBROOK and colophon are registered trademarks of Penguin Random House LLC.

Library of Congress Cataloging-in-Publication Data
Names: Raynor, Jordan, author.
Title: The sacredness of secular work : 4 ways your job matters for eternity
   (even when you're not sharing the Gospel) / Jordan Raynor.
Description: First edition. | Colorado Springs, CO : Waterbrook, 2024. |
   Includes bibliographical references.
Identifiers: LCCN 2023028616 | ISBN 9780593193099 (hardcover : acid free paper) |
   ISBN 9780593193105 (ebook)
Subjects: LCSH: Secularism.
Classification: LCC BL2747.8 .R38 2024 | DDC 248.4—dc23/eng/20230929
LC record available at https://lccn.loc.gov/2023028616

Printed in the United States of America on acid-free paper

waterbrookmultnomah.com

9 8 7 6 5 4 3 2

First Edition

Book design by Jo Anne Metsch

Most WaterBrook books are available at special quantity discounts for bulk purchase for premiums, fundraising, and corporate and educational needs by organizations, churches, and businesses. Special books or book excerpts also can be created to fit specific needs. For details, contact specialmarketscms@penguinrandomhouse.com.

To Tim Keller,

without whom this book would not exist

CONTENTS

INTRODUCTION

What If the Great Commission
Isn't What It's All About?

You're not a pastor, missionary, or religious professional. You're a mere Christian like me who works as an entrepreneur, teacher, or barista. And all your life you've been told implicitly and sometimes explicitly that your work is secular because you're not in "full-time ministry." Believer, nothing could be further from the truth.

The word *secular* means "without God."[1] But we Christians believe that God is with us wherever we go through the power of his Holy Spirit (see 1 Corinthians 6:19). So the only thing you need to do to instantly make your secular workplace sacred is walk through the front door or log on to Zoom.

Now, clearly some work is off-limits for Christ-followers. But I'm going to go ahead and assume that you're not making a living peddling pornography, exploiting the poor, or doing something else that overtly contradicts God's Word. If that's true and you're doing your best to live unto God, then in the words of the great preacher Charles Spurgeon, "Nothing is secular—everything is sacred!"[2]

There's no question of the sacredness of your seemingly secular work, believer. The much more interesting and life-changing question is this: How exactly does your sacred work matter beyond the present? How does it matter for *eternity*?

Because God's Word promises that it does! In 1 Corinthians 15:58, the apostle Paul says this: "Always give yourselves fully to the work of the Lord, because you know that your labor in the Lord is not in vain." *Somehow* it matters for eternity.

Commenting on this verse, N. T. Wright, whom *Newsweek* has called "perhaps the world's leading New Testament scholar,"[3] says that "what you *do* in the present—by painting, preaching, singing, sewing, praying, teaching, building hospitals, digging wells, campaigning for justice, writing poems, caring for the needy, loving your neighbor as yourself—*will last into God's future.*"[4]

That sounds incredible. Almost too good to be true! But Wright's words beg this question: *How?* How is the work I've done as a tech entrepreneur—leading Zoom meetings, building spreadsheets, and selling software—going to "last into God's future"? How is your work driving an Uber, changing a diaper, or writing stories "not in vain"? The purpose of this book is to help you answer that question—to help you see how your so-called "secular" work matters for eternity.*

When I used to hear people tell me that my work as an entrepreneur "matters for eternity," I would think, *Right, because my job gives me the ability to share the gospel with my coworkers and give money to my church and missionaries.* Maybe you've thought the same thing.

---

* This feels like the right time to clarify what I mean by the word *work*. Most obviously, I'm referring to the work you get paid to do. But I'm not *just* referring to your job. Why? Because God defines *work* much more broadly than the things we do for income. His definition of *work* is so broad that in Exodus 20:10 he said that even animals work. I think the most biblical way to define *work*, then, is this: "to expend energy in an effort to achieve a desired result; the opposite of leisure and rest." That definition includes what you do for pay as an analyst, pest controller, or librarian, *as well as* doing laundry, mowing the grass, or studying for an exam. All of this is work. And all of it matters for eternity, as you'll see throughout this book.

This is what I'll refer to as "instrumental value" through-out this book. The idea is that we can leverage our jobs to the instrumental end of obeying Jesus's Great Commission to "make disciples of all nations" (see Matthew 28:19–20). High-light or underline this definition now, as you're going to want to refer back to it:

> **Instrumental Value:** Your work matters for eternity be-cause you can leverage it to share the gospel with those you work with.

Now, our work certainly *does* have instrumental value. But here's the problem: Even if you're great at finding opportuni-ties to make disciples at work, my guess is that 99 percent of your time on the job is spent on tasks other than telling your co-workers about Jesus. If our work has only instrumental value, then the vast majority of the time we spend at work is totally useless in the grand scheme of eternity.

I don't know about you, but I find that *deeply* depressing. More importantly, it's deeply untrue. Dr. Amy Sherman is spot-on when she says that our teaching on the eternal sig-nificance of work is "insufficiently biblical if there's never any mention of the inherent value of the work itself."[5]

The core idea of this book is that in addition to your work having *instrumental value,* it has eternal *intrinsic value* to God.[6] Here's what I mean by that term:

> **Intrinsic Value:** Your work matters for eternity *even when* you're not leveraging it to the instrumental end of sharing the gospel with those you work with.

Why is it so hard to see the intrinsic value of your work? Because the Great Commission has functionally become the only commission that pastors and other religious professionals call Christians to today.

In one of the bestselling books of all time, one pastor says, "The consequences of your mission [and here he's talking exclusively about the Great Commission] will last forever; the consequences of your job will not."[7] Another popular Bible teacher says, "This side of heaven, the *only* investments with eternal significance are people."[8] And in sermon after sermon, preachers exhort us to either *pray* for missionaries, *give* to missionaries, or *go* be missionaries ourselves—with no mention of a fourth option to *stay* and embrace our work as programmers, cooks, and marketers for the glory of God and the good of others.

Pastor John Mark Comer admits that "the church—mine included—has usually focused *way* more on the calling to make disciples" than the other callings of the Christian life.[9] But here's what's fascinating: Turning the Great Commission into the only commission is new in church history. Which raises an interesting question . . .

WHEN DID THE GREAT COMMISSION BECOME THE ONLY COMMISSION?

Short answer? Very, *very* recently. This pervasive idea that evangelism is the only thing Jesus called us to is relatively new in Christian history, which, of course, should make it highly suspect.

Dr. Robbie Castleman says this about the Great Commission text found in Matthew 28: "For the first 1600 years of . . . the life of church, this passage was read and understood . . . not as fanfare for missiology."[10] Three faculty members at the conservative Southeastern Baptist Theological Seminary agree, saying, "Before at least the seventeenth century, the [Great Commission] *was largely ignored* when discussing the church's missional assignment."[11]

Please read that again. Before four hundred years ago, Christians didn't interpret the call to make disciples as the exclusive call on a Christian's life. But somehow, in the last few centuries, we've begun acting like sharing the gospel is the only eternally significant thing we can do, perhaps in part because of the label we've attached to this command, turning it from *a* commission to the singular great one.

But here's what's mind-boggling: The term *Great Commission* isn't even part of the original biblical manuscripts. It's a man-made heading that, as the preface to the NIV Bible warns, is "not to be regarded as part of the biblical text."[12]

And get this: The label *Great Commission* didn't even show up in print until the 1600s. And it wasn't until the late 1800s that the phrase became popular when Hudson Taylor used it to recruit people to serve as missionaries in China.[13] The term *Great Commission* isn't part of the inerrant Word of God. It's simply the catchiest marketing slogan of the modern missions movement.

Now the command itself? That's a different story. Hudson Taylor was right when he said, "The Great Commission is not an option to be considered; it is a command to be obeyed."[14] And my family and I are *deeply* passionate about obeying that command—constantly looking for opportunities to leverage our lives and work to the instrumental end of sharing the gospel with our co-workers, neighbors, and classmates.

The Great Commission is so important that we will spend all of chapter 6 unpacking how to most effectively make disciples in our post-Christian context, as this is clearly *one* of the ways our work matters for eternity. But it's far from the *only* way.

Thankfully, many leaders of the modern missions machine

are beginning to agree. One of those leaders is Andrew Scott, the CEO of Operation Mobilization, a large traditional missions agency, who says, "I may be labeled a heretic here, [but] I actually think that we have overplayed the Great Commission."[15]

I don't think that sounds heretical at all. Based on what we've seen, I think that sounds conservative and orthodox. "The *real* heresy," says my pastor, Chris Basham, "is hurting our people by devaluing the 99% of their lives in which they're not explicitly preaching the gospel."[16]

Lest I be misinterpreted, let me state this as clearly as I can: *The Great Commission is indeed great!* It's just not *only*. And there is great danger in treating it as the only commission Jesus gave us.

FIVE PROBLEMS WITH MAKING THE GREAT COMMISSION THE ONLY COMMISSION

1. Jesus Never Did

Acts 1:3 tells us that after Jesus's resurrection "he appeared to [the apostles] over a period of forty days and spoke about the kingdom of God." I did the math. There are 3,456,000 seconds in forty days. The Great Commission text takes roughly twenty seconds to read out loud. Do you really think Jesus intended for us to interpret what he said in 0.00058 percent of this time as the *exclusive* mission of the church? I don't think so.

But many people argue that the Great Commission should be the be-all and end-all for Christ-followers because the command to make disciples was the last one Jesus spoke before ascending into heaven. But actually, it wasn't. Check out the full passage:

Go and make disciples of all nations, baptizing them in the name of the Father and of the Son and of the Holy Spirit, and teaching them to obey everything I have commanded you. And surely I am with you always, to the very end of the age. (Matthew 28:19–20)

Just to make sure his followers didn't interpret the call to make disciples as the totality of their job description, Jesus told them to teach others to obey *everything* he had commanded them to do. The Gospels record him giving about fifty unique commands.[17] If Jesus meant for us to interpret the call to make disciples as the only commission of the Christian life, he could have said so. But he didn't. Instead, he used his final words to reiterate the importance of following the totality of his teachings.

Here's the second problem with making the Great Commission the only commission.

2. It Leads to a Diminished View of Christ's Redemption

It's not a coincidence that at roughly the same time the Great Commission became the only commission, Christians began preaching an abridged version of the gospel that's all about "Jesus coming to save us from our sins."

In chapter 1, we'll see that while Jesus certainly came "to seek and to save the lost" (Luke 19:10), that was only *part* of his redemptive work. Why? Because in the beginning God created *all* things good before sin made *all* things cursed. And that curse affected more than just people—it affected the earth, economics, aesthetics, culture, and our work.

Jesus came to reverse that curse *in full* and usher in "the renewal of *all* things" (Matthew 19:28). But when all we preach is the church's commission to save souls, it inevitably leads to an implicit (and often explicit) message that the only thing God will save in the end is people.

That, of course, blocks us from seeing the intrinsic value of our work. But much more importantly, it's heresy that diminishes the power of Jesus's death, burial, and resurrection! Randy Alcorn is right: "The breadth and depth of Christ's redemptive work will escape us as long as we think it is limited to humanity."[18]

By turning the Great Commission into the only commission in the last few centuries, we've made it *very* easy to preach an abridged gospel that implies that Jesus's victory was, at best, a partial one. Which, of course, is no victory at all.

That's the second reason why it's so dangerous to treat the Great Commission as the only commission. Here's the third.

3. It Neglects the Other Aspects of the Kingdom

While today we preach almost exclusively the gospel of individual salvation, Jesus preached almost exclusively what he called "[the] gospel of the kingdom" (Matthew 24:14). And as we'll see in chapter 2, God's kingdom contains *far* more than just the King and his subjects. It includes the intangible marks of justice, peace, and love as well as some of the tangible work of our hands!

But when we turn the Great Commission into the only commission, we can easily neglect these other aspects of the kingdom. Justice doesn't matter. Beauty doesn't matter. Cultural excellence doesn't matter. Unless, of course, those things are in vogue at this particular moment in time and can thus be leveraged to the instrumental end of evangelism.

This inevitably leads to the fair accusation that Christians are "so heavenly minded that they are no earthly good."[19]

Which brings me to the fourth problem with functionally making the Great Commission the only commission.

4. Ironically, It Makes Us Less Effective at the Great Commission

For at least three reasons.

First, *it is when Christians are the most earthly good that Christianity becomes the most attractive.* In the words of N. T. Wright,

> It is when the church . . . acts with decisive power in the real world—to build and run a successful school, or medical clinic; to free slaves or remit debts; to establish a housing project . . . or a credit union for those ashamed to go into a bank; to enable drug users and pushers to kick the habit and the lifestyle . . . that people will take the message of Jesus seriously.[20]

Second, *when we turn the Great Commission into the only commission, Christians feel guilty for working in the very places where they're most likely to carry out the Great Commission.*

According to pastor Tim Keller's research, "80% or more of evangelism in the early church was done not by ministers or evangelists" but by mere Christians working as farmers, tentmakers, and mothers.[21] That was true in the early church and is likely to be true for the foreseeable future, as non-Christians are more reticent than ever to darken the door of a church[22] and entire nations are closing their doors to Christian missionaries.[23]

When the Great Commission is the only one we hear preached and when the only people we see on the stages of our churches are pastors and full-time missionaries, we inevitably feel guilty about working anywhere other than the mission field. Most dramatically, that guilt will lead us to leave the very workplaces where we're most likely to make disciples. At a minimum, it will make us half-hearted creatures while we stay there.

I've shared the gospel more in the two years I've been writing this book than in the ten years prior. Why? Because once you understand how 100 percent of your time matters for eternity and not just the 1 percent when you get to explicitly share the gospel, *it makes you come fully alive.* And fully alive people attract the lost like craft coffee attracts hipsters.

Third, *making the Great Commission the only commission creates unbiblical obstacles to following Jesus.*

We've all heard the statistics about young people leaving the church after they graduate high school. Each time one of these studies is published, we *love* to blame "liberals." We *love* to blame "culture." But I think our overemphasis on the Great Commission is partially to blame. Because after our kids "walked the aisle" and "prayed the prayer," we never validated their God-given desires to work for the betterment of this world.

In elevating one of Jesus's commissions to the only Great one, we've told our young people that if they *really* love Jesus, they will move to a mud hut five thousand miles away from home to work as a full-time missionary. But for many, that just doesn't seem like who God made them to be or what he's called them to do. They're *willing* to follow God wherever he might call them, but missions as we've defined it just doesn't seem like their thing. As author Skye Jethani explains,

Young people, perhaps more than previous generations, have a strong sense of their specific callings. They believe God has called them into business, the arts, government, the household, education, the media, the social sector, or health care, and they are often very committed to these venues of cultural engagement. But when their specific callings are not acknowledged by the institutional church . . . the young are unlikely to engage.[24]

And in the most extreme cases, overemphasizing the Great Commission keeps people from ever committing to Christ in the first place!

I was reminded of this recently when a friend told me about his teenage son. This young man admits he's a sinner and believes that Christ's death and resurrection are the only way he can be forgiven of his sins. But he can't seem to confess Jesus as the Lord of his life. When his father asked him why, he replied, "Because I don't think I want to move away from you and Mom to be a missionary."

As I listened to this grieving father share this story, I grew apoplectic. My blood was boiling. Our turning the Great Commission into the only commission has blocked this kid from seeing *how he can even be a Christian* without being a donor-supported missionary!

Tragically, I've heard many more stories just like this one.* This alone is more than enough reason to stop twisting the Great Commission into the only commission. But here's one final reason this distortion of Christian purpose is so problematic.

---

* Want to hear another one? Listen to Jodi Benson (the voice of Ariel in the animated version of *The Little Mermaid*) share how she resisted committing her life to Christ for fear of giving up her career in musical theater: https://podcast .jordanraynor.com/episodes/jodi-benson-voice-of-ariel-in-the-little-mermaid.

5. It Blocks Us from Seeing the Full Extent of How Our Work Matters for Eternity

If the Great Commission is the only commission, then our work has value only when leveraged to the instrumental end of evangelism. And if our work has only instrumental value, then most of us are wasting most of our time.

That's *terribly* disheartening because God has "set eternity in the human heart" (Ecclesiastes 3:11). We all "wanna build something that's gonna outlive" us.[25] We want this life to count for the next one. But if we can't see how that's possible, we lose purpose, hope, and a deep sense of connection with God as we go about our days. Leo Tolstoy, the writer of classics such as *War and Peace,* once said that it was this idea that

> brought me to the point of suicide when I was fifty years old. . . . It is the question without which life is impossible. . . . It is this: what will come of what I do today or tomorrow? . . .
>
> Or expressed another way: is there any meaning in my life that will not be annihilated by the inevitability of death which awaits me?[26]

That is *the* question, isn't it? What *is* the purpose of building a business, working a register, or planning an event if those actions don't lead to an opportunity to share the gospel? Sure, they are means of loving our neighbors as ourselves in the present (see Matthew 22:39). But *beyond* the here and now, how do those actions matter for *eternity*?

That is the question this book will answer. That is our destination. But because of our modern overemphasis on the Great Commission, we're required to travel an unexpected path to answer it.

HOW TO SEE THE BIGGER PICTURE OF HOW YOUR WORK MATTERS FOR ETERNITY

I want you to picture a tree that represents the unbiblical lie that your work matters for eternity only when you leverage it to the instrumental end of sharing the gospel. This tree's growth is fueled by two thick roots that must be severed if we're going to see the intrinsic value of our work.

The first root is what I call "the Abridged Gospel," which has become the *dominant* version of Jesus's good news preached in our churches today. Of course, what we believe about the gospel and what we believe about our purpose are inextricably linked. Which is why, in chapter 1, we'll replace the Abridged Gospel with a more biblical, *un*abridged gospel that ascribes ultimate purpose to our work.

The second root of this lie is an abridged understanding of eternity, or what Jesus called "the kingdom of heaven." Most of us spend more time planning dinner than we do thinking about eternity, leading us to settle for wishy-washy half truths about heaven that are informed more by culture than by Scripture. In chapter 2, we'll replace five of those half truths with whole truths that vastly expand our vision of how our work matters to God.

Those first two chapters make up part 1 of this book, helping us see both the instrumental *and* the intrinsic value of our work—the *dual* commissions we've been called to in the First and Great Commissions. I'll warn you ahead of time: Those chapters may be a bit heady, but they have the potential to *radically* change your life. And I think I've added enough *Hamilton,* Taylor Swift, and Disney Easter eggs to make them easy reads.*

---

* By my count, there are twenty-one of these Easter eggs buried in the book (twelve from *Hamilton,* eight from Taylor, and one from Disney). Why hide

With the foundation of part 1 under our feet, we'll finally be ready to see the full extent of how our work matters for eternity. That's the focus of part 2 of this book, with each chapter diving deep into one of the four most interesting and encouraging ways our work is not in vain.

We'll see that our work has intrinsic and eternal value because it is a vehicle for bringing God pleasure (chapter 3), because it has the power to determine what *physically* lasts into heaven (chapter 4), and because it is largely through our vocations that God's kingdom is revealed on earth as it is in heaven (chapter 5). Finally, in chapter 6, we'll explore how to better leverage our work to the instrumental end of carrying out the Great Commission in our increasingly post-Christian context.

Before we turn to chapter 1, I want to make a promise to you: This book won't just be interesting. It will also be profoundly *helpful*. I won't just tell you how your job matters for eternity. I'll show you how to respond to those truths in order to maximize the eternal impact of your work.

To that end, I encourage you to download the free workbook I've created to accompany this book, which contains space for you to take notes and more than twenty hyperpractical exercises to help you take action on what you read. You can download *The Sacred Response* workbook for free at jordanraynor.com/response.

The British novelist Dorothy Sayers once said, "In nothing has the Church so lost Her hold on reality as in Her failure to understand and respect the secular vocation."[27] Are you ready to see how your seemingly "secular" vocation matters

---

these references instead of explicitly calling them out? To spare the nonfans and to surprise and delight my fellow superfans. I swear, I'm only cryptic and Machiavellian 'cause I care. Happy hunting!

for eternity—*even* the 99 percent of the time you're not explicitly sharing the gospel with your co-workers? Are you ready to be freed from the guilt that comes with being a mere Christian who's not working in "full-time ministry"? Good. Then let's begin!

PART I

Finding Eternal Purpose in the
99 Percent of the Time You're
Not Sharing the Gospel

1

THE UNABRIDGED GOSPEL

Victor Boutros is one of the few entrepreneurs history will remember a hundred years from now. Because there's a decent chance that Boutros and his team at the Human Trafficking Institute (HTI) will decimate modern slavery in our lifetime.

Today approximately twenty-seven million people are victims of sex and labor trafficking—many of them children.[1] And although there are anti-trafficking laws in every country, these heinous crimes continue to thrive because of a lack of enforcement.[2]

Boutros—a former star prosecutor at the U.S. Department of Justice—and his team at HTI are implementing a scalable solution to this problem. By helping governments in developing countries create law enforcement units specializing in human trafficking, HTI has achieved truly extraordinary results. In Uganda alone, HTI's work led to a 225 percent increase in the number of traffickers successfully prosecuted just *one year* after putting boots on the ground.[3]

What motivates Boutros to do this incredible work is his apprenticeship to Jesus Christ, who came "to set the oppressed free" (Luke 4:18). Because of passages like this one, Boutros has no doubt that his work matters for eternity. But many Christians do—a sad fact that Boutros and his fundraising lead, Miles Morrison, have had to confront many times while trying to raise money from fellow believers.

Take the conversation Morrison had with a wealthy Christian we'll call Richard as case in point. After Morrison walked Richard through the impact of HTI's work, the prospective donor was clearly impressed. "It seemed like a perfect meeting," Morrison told me. "I was *certain* Richard was going to write a large check."

But before committing, Richard had one final question: "Now, this is a Christian organization, correct? You all are sharing the gospel with these victims?"

"No," Morrison explained. "While myself, our founder, and many of our team are Christians, we legally *can't* share the gospel with these victims given the official relationship HTI has with our government partners."

That was *not* the answer Richard was looking for. The meeting was over. Richard was out.

"I was flabbergasted," Morrison told me. "But sadly, there are many Christians like Richard who don't see how pulling these kids out of brothels matters to God. It's as if the physical redemption of these kids is totally irrelevant unless it also leads to their spiritual redemption."

As well-intentioned as Richard most certainly was, he had fallen for the lie that the only work of eternal consequence is work that is leveraged to the instrumental end of saving souls.

To debunk that lie, we must address the two thick roots that enable it to grow: an incomplete understanding of the gospel (the subject of this chapter) and an incomplete understanding of the nature of eternity or heaven (the subject of chapter 2). Because what we believe about the gospel is inextricably linked to what we believe about what matters in the grand scheme of eternity.

So we can't be too hard on people like Richard. His decision is one that many Christians would make based on the abridged version of the gospel that dominates many streams of the modern evangelical church. I could cite hundreds of examples of this version of the gospel, but here are just a few.

One influential Christian philanthropist defines the gospel as "the good news that Jesus came to earth to make it possible for all of us to live forever with Him in heaven."[4] A popular Sunday School curriculum tells kids that the entirety of Scripture is "the story of God's plan to save people through Jesus."[5] And in one of the bestselling books of all time, one pastor declares that "[God] wants all his lost children found! That's the *whole reason* Jesus came to earth."[6] In other words, saving you and me is the essence and totality of the gospel.

All these statements are versions of what I call "the Abridged Gospel," which can be summarized like this:

> **The Abridged Gospel:** The gospel is the good news that Jesus came to save people from their sins.

This articulation of the gospel is pervasive throughout Christian sermons, songs, and media today. And while every word of the Abridged Gospel is, of course, *gloriously* true, there are three significant problems with defining the gospel in this way.

THREE PROBLEMS WITH THE ABRIDGED GOSPEL

1. It's Incomplete

The Abridged Gospel distills the good news of God's Word into a two-act drama—humans sinned; Christ redeemed us—and functionally neglects the rest.

I was reminded of this when I visited the Museum of the

Bible and saw an otherwise incredible film that says that the Fall of Genesis 3 is "where our journey begins."[7] All due respect, but no, it's not!

The Abridged Gospel plops us into the middle of the biblical narrative without the essential context of the beginning and end. It's the equivalent of starting the *Star Wars* saga with *Episode VI* and wondering why Luke has daddy issues.

The Abridged Gospel is all about what Jesus has saved us *from*—namely, sin. But without the beginning and end of the story, it's impossible to see what Jesus has saved us *for*. That's the first reason why the Abridged Gospel is so problematic. Here's the second.

2. It's Individualistic

If I wasn't a sucker for alliteration, that would read "*Hyper*-individualistic." The Abridged Gospel is all about us human beings going to heaven when we die—the rest of creation be damned.

It shouldn't surprise us that this truncated version of the gospel has become so pervasive in recent years. Its rise to prominence perfectly corresponds to the most individualistic cultural moment in history, when the "North American 'idol'" is unquestionably "radical individualism."[8]

But as we'll see in this chapter, while we humans may be "the crown jewel of creation,"[9] we are only part of the creation God has redeemed. In the words of pastor Tim Keller, "[The gospel] is not just a wonderful plan for 'my life' but a wonderful plan for the world."[10] And that truth has *enormous* implications for our work.

Here's the third and final problem with the Abridged Gospel.

3. It's Innovative

If a Christian who lived before the 1800s were to hop into a DeLorean, time travel to the present, and hear us define the gospel as "the good news that Jesus came to save people from their sins," they would stare at us in awkward silence, waiting for us to say more.

As many historians have pointed out, the Abridged Gospel is a very recent idea.[11] Dr. Mike Metzger explains that "tragically, two hundred years ago the [biblical] story was edited to two chapters; the *fall* and *redemption*. The opening chapter of creation was largely forgotten. The new starting line was Genesis Three."[12]

I won't bore you with how we got here.* What you need to know is that the Abridged Gospel is new—it's innovative—and, thus, it should be seriously scrutinized.

To reiterate what I said in the introduction, it's not a co-incidence that the Abridged Gospel came to prominence at roughly the same time the Great Commission became the only commission we preach. These two ideas are inseparable! If "the *whole reason* Jesus came to earth" was to save human beings,[13] then your work matters only when you leverage it to the instrumental end of sharing the gospel with other human beings.

So, if we want to see the intrinsic value of our work, we have to catch a bigger, more accurate, more biblical picture of Jesus's good news—the Unabridged Gospel, if you will. Not the abridged two-act version that starts in Genesis 3 and ends at Easter. But the full five acts of God's good news that stretch from Genesis 1 to Revelation 22.

---

* If you're really curious, read chapter 3 of Hugh Whelchel's excellent book *How Then Should We Work?*

As the philosopher Alasdair MacIntyre once said, "I can only answer the question 'What am I to do?' if I can answer the prior question 'Of what story or stories do I find myself a part?'"[14] The Unabridged Gospel answers that question. So go ahead and pour yourself another cup of coffee, and let's dig into that story together.

ACT 1: CREATION (THE GENESIS OF YOUR PURPOSE)

When the Abridged Gospel is the dominant one we preach, our thoughts about God inevitably center on his love, grace, and mercy toward human beings. And while he is certainly all those things and more, it's worth considering that before God told us that he is loving, gracious, or merciful, he told us that he is a God who creates.

It's the very first verb in Scripture: "In the beginning God *created*" (Genesis 1:1). In the beginning God was *productive*. In the beginning God *worked*.

Now, I know what you're thinking: *Come on, Jordan. God didn't work, per se.* Well, his Word says he did! Genesis 2:2 says that "by the seventh day God had finished the *work* he had been doing; so on the seventh day he rested from all his *work*."

And while Genesis 1 shows us God working with his words, Genesis 2 shows him working with his hands, getting "down into the muck" to dig a garden, plant an orchard, and sculpt human bodies (see Genesis 2:7–21).[15] In the words of one commentary, "If the transcendent majesty of God's work in Genesis 1 nonetheless tempts us to think it is not actually work, Genesis 2 leaves us no doubt."[16]*

---

* By the way, the Bible is the only religious text to claim that God works because it is good. Other religions say that the gods formed human beings to work and serve them. Take the Enuma Elish as an example. In that account of the origin of the world, Marduk, the king of the gods, says that humankind "shall

And this matters to our own work today, because family origins matter. *Harry Potter and the Sorcerer's Stone* offers a great picture of this. The story centers on eleven-year-old Harry, who is uncertain about who he is, largely because he knows next to nothing about the parents he lost shortly after his birth. But when a man named Hagrid tells Harry that his parents were great wizards, everything starts to make sense. "Harry—yer a wizard," Hagrid says. "With a mum an' dad like yours, what else would yeh be?"[17]

You see, Harry couldn't understand the work he was called to do until he understood the work of his parents. The same is true with us. And right here, in the first act of Scripture, we see our heavenly Father showing up as a laborer before he showed up as a preacher.

But God's work isn't the end of act 1 of the Unabridged Gospel. Contrary to how Genesis 1 is typically preached, the sixth day wasn't the end of creation—it was just the beginning!* God never intended creation to be a *product* we passively consume. He intended it to be a *project* we actively participate in.[18] We see this explicitly in the Godhead's first words to humankind in Genesis 1:26–28:

be charged with the service of the gods / That they might be at ease!" "The Creation Epic (Enuma Elish)," trans. E. A. Speiser, in *The Ancient Near East: An Anthology of Texts and Pictures,* ed. James B. Pritchard (Princeton, N.J.: Princeton University Press, 2011), 33. Work is beneath the gods of other religions. But not the one true God of the Bible.

* As I say in my children's book *The Creator in You,* "And now you might think that our story is ending, but in fact this is just the beginning. God made you to *look* like Him—to act and work and *create* with Him. Because while in six days God created a lot, there are so many things that He simply did not—like bridges and baseballs, sandcastles and s'mores. God asked *us* to create and fill the planet with more." Jordan Raynor, *The Creator in You* (Colorado Springs, Colo.: Water-Brook, 2022).

Then God said, "Let us make mankind in our image, in our likeness, so that they may rule over the fish in the sea and the birds in the sky, over the livestock and all the wild animals, and over all the creatures that move along the ground."

So God created mankind in his own image,
    in the image of God he created them;
    male and female he created them.

God blessed them and said to them, "Be fruitful and increase in number; fill the earth and subdue it."

If you want to see how your work matters for eternity beyond the important and instrumental end of carrying out the Great Commission, this is where you must start. Because this right here is God's original intent for humankind. The *First* Commission he gave to you and me. This is our job description.

First, we're called to *"be fruitful and increase in number."*

This command is pretty straightforward. God wants us to have lots of babies and spread out across the earth. Enough said.

Second, God commands us to *"fill the earth."*

Scholars agree that this isn't God reiterating the call for us to fill the maternity ward.[19] While the command to "increase in number" is a call to procreation, the command to "fill the earth" is a call to civilization and cultural creation.[20] It's God's call to take this largely blank canvas he handed us on the sixth day and fill it with art and architecture, schools and services, tree forts and telescopes. All of this falls under the banner of "fill the earth."[21]

The third component of our First Commission is to *"subdue"* the earth.

Wayne Grudem, general editor of the *ESV Study Bible,* explains that this word means "to make the earth useful for human beings' benefit and enjoyment."[22] That sounds a lot like the work most of us do every day as engineers, musicians, and city planners, doesn't it? I don't know if Nike co-founder Phil Knight is a Christian, but I *do* know that he understands the God-ordained call to subdue better than most. Knight writes,

> When you make something, when you improve something, when you deliver something, when you add some new thing or service to the lives of strangers, making them happier, or healthier, or safer, or better, and when you do it all crisply and efficiently, smartly, the way everything should be done but so seldom is— you're participating more fully in the whole grand human drama.[23]

Amen. And you're doing the very thing God created you to do.

Here's the fourth and final command we need to understand in God's First Commission to humankind: the command to *"rule."*

Now, God isn't asking us to exploit the earth and other image-bearers as so many rulers do today. That's not the idea here. As one Hebrew scholar helpfully explains, the word *rule* means "to actively partner with God in taking the world somewhere."[24]

I want you to stop for a second to consider the *absurdity* of God's goodness here. God could have filled, subdued, and ruled this world all on his own. But Genesis makes clear that that was never his intent. In his inimitable grace, God left this world mostly empty and invited you and me to fill and steward it, setting up a theme that we will see throughout the Unabridged Gospel—namely, that God chooses to work in this world primarily *through you and me.*

Does God work unilaterally? Of course! But we are the *"primary* instrument" through which he works.[25] We are what Martin Luther calls "the masks of God," working with him to fill, subdue, and rule creation on his behalf.[26] And the origin of that truth is found right here in Genesis 1. In the words of N. T. Wright,

> Creation, it seems, was not a tableau, a static scene. It was designed as a *project,* created in order to go somewhere. The creator has a future in mind for it; and Human—this strange creature, full of mystery and glory—is the means by which the creator is going to take his project forward.[27]

But forward to *where* exactly? What is the end toward which we—God's co-workers—were originally meant to strive? Put simply, to take the garden and turn it into "a garden city"—the eternal kingdom of God (aka the kingdom of heaven).[28] Right here in act 1 of the biblical drama, we see the genesis of our purpose: to partner with God to implement his sovereign rule on earth as it is in heaven.

There's a largely overlooked detail in Genesis 2 that perfectly symbolizes this truth. Genesis 2:10–12 says, "A river watering the garden flowed from Eden. . . . It winds through the entire land of Havilah, where there is gold. (The gold of that land is good; aromatic resin and onyx are also there.)"

So, in the second chapter of Scripture, we find three elements near Adam and Eve's worksite: gold, aromatic resin (which can be translated "pearls"), and onyx (which, for those of us who aren't geologists, is a beautiful stone).[29] Where else do we see these three things in God's Word? In the second to last chapter of Scripture, which describes the New Jerusalem, God's eternal city, as having streets of gold, gates made of pearls, and foundations "decorated with every kind of precious stone," including—wait for it—onyx (see Revelation 21:18–21).

In his excellent book *Art and Faith,* Makoto Fujimura conjectures that "these materials . . . were beneath the ground to be discovered by Adam and Eve or by their descendants for the construction of what would become the city of God."[30]

I think that's exactly right. I think this is God's poetic way of illustrating the First Commission. It's his way of saying, "Hey, kids: I created this world for you to fill, subdue, and rule with me, for my glory and your joy. And somehow all your labor will not be in vain. Just wait and see. I'm going to take your work and use it to build our eternal home."

Do you see how *epic* the biblical narrative is? The purpose of your life isn't something as small and fleeting as your happiness. The purpose of your life is to participate in the ultimate cosmic drama—working with God to cultivate heaven on earth. "Forget 'happiness'; you are called to a *throne.*"[31]

There's a scene in *Tangled* when Rapunzel puts on a crown, looks in the mirror, and realizes to her shock that *she's* the lost princess of her kingdom.[32] Believer, I hope you're starting to see that *you're* the lost princess or prince of *the* kingdom, created by the Way Maker to be a world maker on his behalf.

We're almost ready to move on to act 2 of the Unabridged Gospel. But before we do, let me share the first of twelve propositions I'll lay down in this chapter and the next about how your work has intrinsic value to God. Based on what we've seen in act 1, we can confidently state the following:

Proposition 1: Your work has intrinsic value because God works for the pure joy of it.

God had no need to work. So we can assume that he worked for the pure joy of it. And if God worked for the pure joy of it, his children can too. In the words of pastor Tom Nelson, "As image-bearers of God, who is a worker, we must remember that our work has intrinsic value in itself."[33]

Proposition 2: Your work has intrinsic value because God deems both the spiritual and the material realms good.

After each of the first six days of creation, God looked at his work and saw that it was "good" (see Genesis 1). And contrary to what proponents of the Abridged Gospel might imply, God didn't recognize just human beings as good. He determined that the trees, stars, food, lions, tigers, and bears were "good" too. And if God deems these material things good, then we can deem *working* with these things intrinsically good. Here's how one commentary on Genesis 1 articulates this idea:

> There is simply no support . . . for the notion, which somehow entered Christian imagination, that the world is irredeemably evil and the only salvation is an escape into an immaterial spiritual world, much less for the notion that while we are on earth we should spend our time in "spiritual" tasks rather than "material" ones. There is no divorce of the spiritual from the material in God's good world.[34]

And so, a Christian is free to design websites, build houses, or explore outer space, all to God's greater glory.

One more proposition before we move on to act 2:

Proposition 3: Your work has intrinsic value because it's what God created you to do from the beginning.

Remember, the call to fill, subdue, and rule this world with God and for his glory is the *First* Commission on your life. And as we'll soon see, it's the only commission that will never end. So, as Dr. James Davison Hunter says, "The task of world-making has a validity of its own because it is work that God ordained to humankind at creation."[35]

I hope you're starting to see why it's so important to begin our preaching of the gospel here in Genesis 1 and 2. But just to be sure, here's Dr. Sandra Richter to say it explicitly:

I am unable to share the gospel without speaking of Eden. Because when we ask the salvation question, what we are really asking is, what did the first Adam lose? And when we answer the salvation question, what we are really attempting to articulate is, what did the Second Adam (i.e., Jesus) buy back?[36]

Clearly, humankind has lost *a lot* since Eden. Act 1 of the Unabridged Gospel says that God's original intent was for us to dwell with him on a perfect earth and to join the family business: filling, subduing, and ruling the world. If the gospel is going to be truly good news, this has to be our starting point. It sets the scene for the entire tale. It's the beginning of our story *and* a glimpse of the story's ending.

But like any other compelling narrative, this beautiful story is about to take a turn for the worse.

ACT 2: FALL (THE SOURCE OF YOUR FRUSTRATION)

As we transition from act 1 to act 2 of the Unabridged Gospel, we go from glorious light to tragic darkness, like moving from a Narnian summer to never-ending winter, or from Taylor Swift's bubbly *1989* to the grungy *Reputation*.

In Genesis 3, the serpent snuck in through the garden gate, Adam and Eve committed the first sin, and in just nineteen verses the shalom of Genesis 1 and 2 was shattered. Because now the entire world was rightly under God's curse. Here's the account from Genesis 3:16–19:

To the woman [God] said,

"I will make your pains in childbearing very severe;
    with painful labor you will give birth to children.
Your desire will be for your husband,
    and he will rule over you."

To Adam he said, "Because you listened to your wife and ate fruit from the tree about which I commanded you, 'You must not eat from it,'

"Cursed is the ground because of you;
    through painful toil you will eat food from it
    all the days of your life.
It will produce thorns and thistles for you,
    and you will eat the plants of the field.
By the sweat of your brow
    you will eat your food
until you return to the ground,
    since from it you were taken;
for dust you are
    and to dust you will return."

This is likely a very familiar passage to you. So just in case you skimmed over it (no judgment here, I promise), I want to draw your attention to this truth embedded in the passage: The curse broke much more than just our relationship with God. It broke *everything* God deemed good in act 1—human beings, the nonhuman world, *and* the world of work.

Now, because work existed prior to the curse, we know that it was once perfect bliss.* As we saw in act 1, the First Commission was part of God's *blessing* to humankind (see Genesis 1:28). Work was God's first *gift* to his children. For Adam and Eve, "Paradise wasn't a vacation—it was a vocation."[37]

But now, because of the curse, our work "to make the earth useful" and beautiful is difficult and arduous.[38] "Thorns and thistles" fight back against us, and Sunday nights are filled with dread over the impending "case of the Mondays."[39]

But highlight this now, because this distinction is absolutely critical: Genesis 1–3 makes it clear that work is not *the* curse. It *is* cursed as a result of Adam and Eve's sin.

But even though work is now under the curse, God *never once* retracted the First Commission. In fact, he *reiterated* it, most notably after the great Flood. Shortly after Noah and his family hopped off the ark, "God blessed Noah and his sons, saying to them, 'Be fruitful and increase in number and fill the earth'" (Genesis 9:1).

The language here is nearly identical to God's words to Adam and Eve in Genesis 1, but there are some significant differences. Most notable is that while the call to "fill the earth" was reiterated, the command to "rule" was omitted.

---

* In fact, the Hebrew word *abad,* which we translate as "work" in Genesis 2:15, is translated as "worship" in Exodus 3:12. Work and worship were one and the same before the Fall and will be once again on the New Earth. More on that in chapter 2.

Why? Because human beings had been temporarily stripped of much of the authority God delegated to them in act 1.

As we saw in Genesis 1, God's original intent was that we would be his co-rulers—princes and princesses that rightfully represent our King. But in Genesis 3, "instead of carrying out his kingly mandate to rule the world under God, [Adam] joins the Serpent in rebellion against God and attempts to take the crown for himself."[40] But God wouldn't stand for our attempt at a coup d'état, so here in act 2, he took back some of the authority he delegated to us in the beginning. (Until act 4, that is. Stay tuned!)

But even though Noah and his immediate descendants were incapable of fully serving as God's vice-regents, the Lord still reissued much of the First Commission in the context of his blessing. After the Fall, the First Commission was *edited,* but it wasn't *canceled*. Work is still ordained and blessed by God, and thus, it's still intrinsically good.

So good, in fact, that the command to work even made the Ten Commandments! We rightfully view the fourth commandment as a directive to rest and "remember the Sabbath day," but don't forget that it's *also* a command to "labor and do all your work" the other six days (see Exodus 20: 8–11).

Beyond the fourth commandment, Scripture mentions work more than eight hundred times—most of those mentions, of course, coming after the Fall. As Hugh Whelchel points out, "That's more than every mention of worship, music, praise, and singing *combined*."[41] Clearly our work matters to God.

How does all of this help us see the eternal significance of our work beyond leveraging our jobs to the instrumental end of sharing the gospel? Here's our next proposition:

Proposition 4: Your work has intrinsic value because God commands and blesses it even after the Fall.

When we treat the Great Commission as the only commission, we accuse God of needing a plan B. We think, sure, plan A was the First Commission to "fill the earth and subdue it" (Genesis 1:28), but now that sin has entered the world, God has been forced to scrap plan A and replace it with plan B—saving as many souls as possible and getting us all the heck out of this God-forsaken world.

But everything we've just seen totally dismantles that thinking. The sovereign God of the universe doesn't need or desire a plan B. He still takes delight in watching his children lean into plan A—the First Commission to model his creative character by filling the earth and making it more useful. Which is *exactly* what you do today as an architect, server, or project manager.

But again, while we could fill and cultivate the earth after the Fall, we could in no way fulfill God's original intent to rule the earth on his behalf. We couldn't even rule ourselves— a truth painfully revealed on nearly every page of the Old Testament. On this side of Eden, we are all in desperate need of a Redeemer to save us and restore us fully to the First Commission.

In his incomparable mercy and grace, God promised that Redeemer right here in act 2. God told Satan that while he would "strike [the] heel" of this Redeemer, the Chosen One would "crush [Satan's] head" (Genesis 3:15).

But for that Redeemer to prove victorious, he had to win back *everything* sin broke in act 2. His redemption had to spread "far as the curse is found."[42] And that is precisely what we see Jesus accomplish in act 3 of the Unabridged Gospel.

ACT 3: REDEMPTION (THE PURPOSE OF YOUR SALVATION)

Before it became clear that Jesus was the Redeemer that God promised in act 2 of the biblical drama, what most people knew about him was that he was a carpenter or stonemason (see Mark 6:3).[43] Scholars believe that Jesus likely spent his days "negotiating bids, securing supplies, completing projects, and contributing to family living expenses."[44] In other words, Jesus of Nazareth spent most of his life working a regular j-o-b.

Since we know Jesus's ultimate purpose in life, this truth should stop us in our tracks. God could have chosen for Jesus to grow up in anybody's home. He could have placed him in a priestly household, where he would have spent his days in prayer. He could have chosen for him to grow up in the home of a Pharisee, where he would have devoted hours to studying the Scriptures. But instead, God intentionally placed Jesus in the home of a tradesman named Joseph, where he would spend the majority of his time making things with his hands.[45]

Those who preach the Abridged Gospel will find Jesus's occupation surprising but ultimately insignificant. But those of us on a quest to see how our work matters for eternity via the Unabridged Gospel will see Jesus's vocation as *incredibly* significant and one of the *least* surprising parts of his entire life. Why? Because the work of Jesus's *earthly* father wasn't all that different from the work of his *heavenly* one. Here in act 3, Jesus, "the image of the invisible God" (Colossians 1:15), is simply reflecting the character of God the Father in act 1, presenting himself as a laborer first and a preacher second.

But of course, Jesus didn't come to earth just to make Nazareth's finest kitchenettes. He came to make a new world—to redeem everything sin had broken in act 2. And while that certainly includes people (see Luke 19:10), it doesn't *just* include people.

Jesus could have exclusively preached the good news that he came to save people from their sins, but he didn't. He preached what he called "[the] gospel of the kingdom" (Matthew 24:14), referring to his kingdom roughly *ten times* more frequently than the salvation of individual people.[46] As theologian Anthony Hoekema explains, "The kingdom of God . . . does not mean merely the salvation of certain individuals. . . . It means nothing less than the complete renewal of the entire cosmos."[47]

There's a famous line in *The Lord of the Rings* in which Sam asks Gandalf if "everything sad" is "going to come untrue" in the end.[48] The Abridged Gospel says no—only human death will come untrue. The Unabridged Gospel emphatically answers Sam's question in the affirmative. Yes, Sam, everything sad is going to come untrue: death, injustice, smog, scarcity, dilapidated strip malls—*everything.*

And it's that work of renewing all things that we see Jesus previewing in his miracles. Yes, Jesus renewed the *spiritual* realm by driving out demons (see Matthew 8:28–34), but he also began restoring the *material* world. He turned water into wine (see John 2:1–11). He created abundance where there was once a scarcity of food (see Matthew 14:13–21). He saw injustice in the world, and he corrected it (see John 8:2–11). According to Jesus, "the kingdom of God is at hand" to transform the world from top to bottom—sacred *and* secular, spiritual *and* material (Mark 1:15, ESV).

But somehow this lie has entered modern Christian thinking that the material realm of wine, books, and the work of our hands is evil and irredeemable while the spiritual world of human souls alone is good and worth saving.* Summarizing this idea, one pastor says, "There are only two things that last eternally: God's Word and people. Everything else is going to burn up."[49]

Again, I won't lull you to sleep by explaining how our theology got so out of whack here.† What you need to know is this: The idea that Jesus came only to save human beings is an egregious lie—and an incredibly dangerous one for at least two reasons.

First, *it heretically diminishes the power of Christ's death and resurrection.*

Because if Jesus didn't redeem all things, then his redemption is incomplete. Think about it: If God deemed *all* things good in act 1 and if sin corrupted *all* things in act 2, then Jesus would have had to redeem *all* things in act 3 in order for God to make good on his promise that the Savior would crush Satan's head in total victory. As one theologian pointedly says, "If redemption does not go as far as the curse of sin, then God has failed."[50]

To say that the whole reason Jesus came was to save human beings is to diminish the power of the Cross. It's calling Jesus a *loser* instead of *Lord,* because it means that Satan has achieved at least a partial victory. But he hasn't! Christ's death and res-

---

* Fun fact: The word *spiritual* doesn't even show up in the Old Testament. Pastor John Mark Comer explains why: "Because in a Hebrew worldview, *all of life is spiritual.* . . . I think if you had asked Jesus about his spiritual life, he would have looked at you very confused. My guess is he would have asked, What do you mean by my spiritual life? You mean my *life*? All of my life is spiritual." John Mark Comer, *Garden City: Work, Rest, and the Art of Being Human* (Grand Rapids, Mich.: Zondervan, 2015), 97. Which is what led Paul to remind his Padawan Timothy that "everything God created is good, and nothing is to be rejected if it is received with thanksgiving" (1 Timothy 4:4).

† If you're really curious, read the appendix about Christoplatonism in Randy Alcorn's extraordinary book *Heaven.*

urrection were sufficient to redeem the spiritual *and* the material world.

Second, *to say that Jesus came only to save human souls blocks our ability to see the full extent of how our work matters for eternity.*

If God's Word and people are the only things that aren't going to burn up in the end, then the work you do with the material world as a sales rep, landscaper, or brewer matters *only* if you leverage it to the spiritual and instrumental end of sharing the gospel with your co-workers. But because Christ has redeemed *all* things—spiritual and material—you can be confident that the purpose of your life is far greater.

So what is the purpose of your life and work? What is the purpose of your salvation? Paul answers that question explicitly in Ephesians 2:8–10:

> It is by grace you have been saved, through faith—and this is not from yourselves, it is the gift of God—not by works, so that no one can boast. For we are God's handiwork, created in Christ Jesus to do good works, which God prepared in advance for us to do.

So, while we haven't been saved *by* our works, we have been saved *to do* "good works, which God prepared in advance for us to do." And get this: The Greek word *ergon,* which we translate as "works" in this passage, does *not* mean exclusively "spiritual" tasks like evangelism and prayer. According to every biblical concordance I've read, it means "work, task, employment."[51]

This has *tremendously* practical implications for you, believer. Paul is *not* saying that your salvation necessitates quitting your job to do the more "spiritual" work of a pastor or full-time missionary. In fact, in 1 Corinthians 7:20 he says the exact *opposite,* encouraging Christians to "remain in the situation they were in when God called them"—to stay in their roles working as farmers, carpenters, and tentmakers.

And do what while they're in those roles? The "good works . . . God prepared in advance for [them] to do." Now, I know what you're probably wondering: *What exactly are those good works, Jordan?* We'll answer that question in act 4. But before we do, let me quickly spell out how act 3 of the Unabridged Gospel helps us see the eternal value of our work beyond sharing the gospel with those we work with.

> **Proposition 5:** Your work has intrinsic value because Jesus, the Son of God, spent the majority of his life working a regular j-o-b.

> **Proposition 6:** Your work has intrinsic value because Jesus came to save more than the spiritual realm of human souls.

> **Proposition 7:** Your work has intrinsic value because part of the very purpose of your salvation is to do good works.

Not less than evangelism, but certainly much more than evangelism! And in act 4, we'll gain greater clarity as to the end and aim of the good works God prepared for us to do today.

ACT 4: RENEWAL (YOUR DUAL COMMISSIONS)

As we saw in act 3 of the Unabridged Gospel, the coming of the eternal kingdom of God was the dominant theme of Jesus's preaching. Which raises this question: If it was within Jesus's power to reveal his kingdom in full at the Resurrection, why didn't he?

After all, that's certainly what his disciples were expecting. After the Resurrection, they asked Jesus, "Lord, are you at this time going to restore the kingdom to Israel?" (Acts 1:6). Check out Jesus's reply:

> He said to them: "It is not for you to know the times or dates the Father has set by his own authority. But you will receive power when the Holy Spirit comes on you; and you will be my witnesses in Jerusalem, and in all Judea and Samaria, and to the ends of the earth."
>
> After he said this, he was taken up before their very eyes, and a cloud hid him from their sight. (Acts 1:7–9)

Like many Christians today, the disciples were obsessed with knowing exactly when God's kingdom would be revealed in full. But in his final words before his ascension, Jesus turned the disciples' attention away from the *timing* of the kingdom and toward a *task*—specifically, the task of serving as Jesus's witnesses.

Expounding on the original Greek of this passage, Tim Keller explains that the word *witnesses* means "more than simply winning people to Christ":

> The church is to be an agent of the kingdom. It is not only to model the healing of God's rule but it is to spread it . . . ordering lives and relationships and institutions and communities according to God's authority to bring in the blessedness of the kingdom.[52]

Authority is the key word because, here in act 4, Jesus is returning the crown that was rightfully taken from us in act 2. He is fully restoring us to the First Commission to fill, subdue, and *rule* the earth on God's behalf. While "all authority in heaven and on earth has been given to [Christ]" (Matthew 28:18), our King is choosing once again to delegate that authority to his princes and princesses. While Christ has *inaugurated* the eternal kingdom of God, he has given you and me the task of *implementing* it.[53]

For those of us who have grown up with nonstop news at our fingertips, it can be difficult to understand the gap between the inauguration of a kingdom and its implementation. But remember, in previous centuries a new political leader rising to power or signing a law wasn't enough to change the world. People loyal to that sovereign had to physically go throughout the land to proclaim the good news that "a change is gonna come."[54]

Take the Emancipation Proclamation as an example. President Lincoln signed the order to free slaves on January 1, 1863, but it would be another *two and a half years* before slaves in Texas would hear the news and walk away from their masters.[55] There was a gap between the legal reality of Lincoln's achievement and its implementation.

So it is with the kingdom of God. And to the disciples' shock and ours, Jesus said that his kingdom will be implemented, at least in part, *through you and me.* The kingdom of God (aka the kingdom of heaven) isn't going to come in one fell swoop. It's going to come slowly like a mustard seed that takes its time growing into a giant tree or like yeast that's gradually folded into sixty pounds of flour (see Luke 13:18–21).

Which makes perfect sense given the context of the Unabridged Gospel! Because as you now well know, this is exactly how God has been working since the beginning of this drama.

There's a beautiful little detail in John's account of the Resurrection that symbolically ties this all together. In John 20, we're told that upon seeing the resurrected Christ, Mary Magdalene didn't recognize him. She mistook him for "the gardener" (see John 20:11–16).

Now, Jesus had just beaten death. Clearly he could have chosen to be mistaken for *anything*—a carpenter, a fisherman, a great king. But instead, he chose to be mistaken for a gardener. Why? Was it simply because he was raised in the garden tomb?[56] Maybe. But I think the God who created thirty-four thousand species of fish is a bit more creative than that.[57]

Scholars suggest that by including this detail of Mary mistaking Jesus for the gardener, John is alluding to something quite deliberately.[58] He is contrasting Jesus, the Last Adam in act 4, with the first Adam in act 1 (see 1 Corinthians 15:45).

Think about it: In the beginning God inaugurated the world, but he didn't finish it. Instead, he "put [Adam] in the Garden of Eden to work it and take care of it" (Genesis 2:15)— to take this garden and rule it, subdue it, and fill it with heaven on earth. But the first Adam broke God's commandment, ensuring our need for a Redeemer.

Fast-forward thousands of years, and here at the Resurrection, God inaugurated a whole new world. And the Last Adam chose to appear as a gardener as a symbolic way of saying that he is planting heaven on earth once again. And just as the first Adam had his bride, Eve, to help him cultivate the first creation, Jesus, the Last Adam, has his bride, the church, to help him cultivate the final one.

I don't know about you, but the first time I saw that connection, my mind was *blown*. I looked more stunned than a kid seeing Santa for the first time in real life. But not only do we have symbolic evidence for this idea that we help Jesus the Gardener cultivate heaven on earth; we also find explicit evidence for it in the parable of the weeds:

Jesus told them another parable: "The kingdom of heaven is like a man who sowed good seed in his field. . . .

"The one who sowed the good seed is the Son of Man. The field is the world, and the good seed stands for the people of the kingdom." (Matthew 13:24, 37–38)

Jesus couldn't have been any clearer. The kingdom isn't coming in a flash. Jesus the Gardener has scattered his people far and wide to help him implement it. We aren't "waiting on a miracle."[59] "The miracle is *you*."[60]

Or more accurately, the Holy Spirit *in* you. Because while Jesus has given us the *authority* to rule, the Holy Spirit gives us the *power* to do so (see Acts 1:8). Which is precisely why Paul says that "creation waits in eager expectation for the children of God to be revealed" (Romans 8:19). Because it is partially through the Spirit working through the children of God that the kingdom will come "on earth as it is in heaven" (Matthew 6:10).

Now we're finally ready to answer the question we posed at the end of act 3: What are the "good works . . . God prepared in advance for us to do" (Ephesians 2:10)? In short, *the work he intended for us to do from the very beginning!* As professor Nancy Pearcey says, "Redemption is not just about being saved *from* sin, it is also about being saved *to* something—to resume the task for which we were originally created."[61]

And what have we seen is that task? Partnering with God to cultivate heaven on earth. You see, the good news of the gospel is not just that I get to go to heaven *when* I die but that I get to partner with God in revealing heaven on earth *until* I die.

I promise to show you soon what that looks like practically

(especially in chapters 2 and 5). For now, just know that the "good works . . . God prepared in advance for us to do" in act 4 of the Unabridged Gospel are essentially the good works he called us to in act 1: the First Commission—partnering with God to fill, subdue, and rule this world for his glory and the good of others.

But while the work we're called to today is similar to the work humankind was called to in the beginning, it's different in at least two significant ways.

First, *because sin still mars the world, our work today will have a bent toward renewal.*

Adam and Eve had nothing to renew in Eden, because nothing was broken prior to the Fall. There was no need for doctors, police officers, or therapists. So while, through the power of the Spirit, we can once again "become entrepreneurial partners with [God] in advancing his purposes in the world," on this side of Eden we're going to have messes to clean up along the way.[62]

Second, *while our salvation allows us to once again participate fully in the First Commission, today you and I are also called to the Great Commission.*

Again, Jesus's call to be his witnesses in Acts 1:8 doesn't *just* mean evangelism, but it certainly *includes* evangelism! To re-quote Hudson Taylor, "The Great Commission is not an option to be considered; it is a command to be obeyed."[63] And clearly, leveraging your job to the instrumental end of making disciples of Jesus Christ is one of the ways your work is not in vain (much more on this in chapter 6).

But at the risk of beating this poor dead horse to a pulp, *please* don't make the mistake of believing that this is the *only* way your work matters for eternity. The reality is that we now have a *dual* commission. Pastor John Mark Comer explains,

Not one, but two callings.

The original calling—to rule over the earth. To make culture.

And a new calling—to make disciples. . . .

The new calling to make disciples does not negate or cancel out the original calling to create culture. It's a both/and.[64]

And there's a sense in which the Great Commission is a *subset* of the First Commission. Just as human beings were only *part* of the creation God called good in act 1, *part* of what was cursed in act 2, and *part* of what Jesus redeemed in act 3, so the Great Commission to share the gospel is only *part* of our broader commission in act 4 to join Jesus the Gardener in implementing his kingdom.

How does all of this help us see the intrinsic value of our work? Here's our next proposition:

Proposition 8: Your work has intrinsic value because God has called you to a dual vocation: the Great *and* First Commissions.

The call to make disciples *and* the call to partner with Jesus the Gardener to make the kingdom come "on earth as it is in heaven" (Matthew 6:10).

ACT 5: CONSUMMATION (THE END OF ONE STORY AND THE BEGINNING OF THE NEXT)

Take a deep breath. We've come a *long* way in just a few pages. But before we close out this chapter, we have to quickly touch on the fifth and final act of the Unabridged Gospel.

Because while you and I are called to *participate* in the work of implementing the kingdom, "the good news is that God the master craftsman is responsible for *finishing* the work."[65] And he *will* when he fully removes the veil between heaven and earth in the fifth and final act of history, consummating the long-awaited marriage between God's dimension and ours (see Revelation 21–22).

We'll examine that marriage in detail in the next chapter, but before we do, let's quickly summarize the contrast between the Abridged Gospel and the Unabridged Gospel.

The Abridged Gospel: The gospel is the good news that Jesus came to save people from their sins.

The Unabridged Gospel: God created a perfect world and invited his children to rule over it with him and for him. We sinned, ushering in the curse that broke every part of that perfect creation, ensuring our need for a Savior. Jesus's resurrection proved emphatically that he is that Savior who saves us by grace through faith. And while we're not saved *by* our works, we have been saved *for* the good works he prepared for us to do all along: partnering with him to cultivate heaven on earth until he returns to finish the job. Then the triune God will finally dwell with us again on a New Earth, where we will rule with him for ever and ever.

If paragraph summaries aren't your thing, here's a table summarizing the Unabridged Gospel:

Act	Our Mission is	Our Work is	All of Creation is
1: Creation	First Commission	Perfect	Perfect
2: Fall	Truncated First Commission	Good but Painful	Broken
3: Redemption	First Commission + Great Commission	Good but Painful	Redeemed
4: Renewal	First Commission + Great Commission	Good but Painful	Being Renewed
5: Consummation	First Commission	Perfect	Perfect

As I hope you now see, the way we articulate the gospel is *directly* tied to our view of what work matters for eternity. If the Abridged Gospel is the whole of God's good news, then the Great Commission is the only commission that matters in the grand scheme of things. The only way your work is not in vain is if you leverage your role as an athlete, hairdresser, or photographer to the instrumental end of sharing the gospel.

But with the Unabridged Gospel in view, we can now understand and embrace our dual vocation: the Great Commission to make disciples and the First Commission to make an entire world for God's greater glory. And so, our work has instrumental *and* intrinsic value because it's what God created us to do, what he saved us to do, and what we will be doing for all eternity.

But to fully understand and appreciate that truth, we need to replace the half truths many of us have been taught about the very nature of eternity (what Jesus called "the kingdom of heaven") with whole truths that have a direct impact on our vision for our work. That's the subject of the next chapter.

YOUR SACRED RESPONSE

My prayer is not just that this book would be *interesting* but that it would also be *helpful* in leading you to maximize the eternal impact of your work. So, at the end of each chapter, I'm going to ask you to respond to what you've read by working through a single practice. Here's the first one.

In this chapter, we broke down the various components of the First Commission, which God handed down to humankind in Genesis 1:28. Identify the element of this job description that best describes the work you do today:

fill the earth: create good things
subdue: make the earth more useful for human beings' benefit and enjoyment
rule: implement God's sovereign rule on earth as it is in heaven

Now answer these two questions:

1. How do you live out this element of the First Commission in your current job?
2. How does knowing that this is the thing God *created* you to do in act 1 of the Unabridged Gospel and the thing he *redeemed* you to do in act 3 help you see the sacredness of your seemingly secular work?

You'll find space to write out your answers in *The Sacred Response* workbook, which you can download for free at jordanraynor.com/response. There you'll also find an additional practice to help you check for symptoms of the curse in your work today.

HALF TRUTHS ABOUT HEAVEN

Joni Eareckson Tada stared out at the Chesapeake Bay, a life of limitless possibilities ahead of her. Seconds later, the seventeen-year-old's spine and dreams were shattered as she dove headfirst into the floor of the bay.

As her sister carried her toward dry land, Tada realized that she had lost all movement in her arms and legs. Soon she'd hear the devastating news that she would be a quadriplegic confined to a wheelchair and the help of others for the rest of her life.

Understandably, the news sent Tada into a season of deep depression. As Tada recalls in her bestselling memoir, "How I wished for strength and control enough in my fingers to do something, anything, *to end my life*."[1]

But she couldn't. So she begged a friend to assist her in putting an end to the pain. When her friend refused, Tada realized that "all I could do was wait and hope for some hospital accident to kill me."[2]

But God had other plans for Tada. And part of those plans was to use art to give her hope and a future. Of course, Tada couldn't create with her hands, but her occupational therapist suggested she try to draw and paint with her mouth.

Reluctantly, Tada agreed to give it a shot. Holding a stylus between her teeth, she swiveled her head back and forth and up and down until she eked out a simple "line drawing of a cowboy and horse" on some clay.[3] Looking back on that moment, Tada says, "For the first time in almost a year and a half, I was able to express myself in a productive, creative way. It was exciting and gave me renewed hope."[4]

That moment was a seed that blossomed into one of the most unlikely and remarkable art careers imaginable. Tada's art has become famous the world over, earning her the respect of multiple American presidents, and more public appearances than you can count.[5]

In an interview, Larry King once asked Tada to describe the hardest part of painting with one's mouth. "The hardest thing to do is to paint big," Tada said, which makes sense given that the size of her canvases is limited to the range of motion in her neck.[6]

But listen to what Tada told King next: "I can't wait for heaven to get hands that work and feet that walk, and I'll not only jump up, dance, kick, do aerobics, *but I'll paint big splashy murals.*"[7]

Based on the modern caricature of heaven as a glorified retirement home in the sky, Tada's dream sounds sweet but far-fetched—"sentimental hogwash," in the words of Henry F. Potter.[8] But if Tada is right and heaven includes the work of our own hands, then that would have *significant* implications for our understanding of how much our work matters for eternity.*

In part 1 of this book, we've been confronting the unbiblical lie that the only work of eternal consequence is that which we leverage to the instrumental end of evangelism. As I've

---

* By the way, if you want to listen to Tada go into *beautiful* detail about her vision for her paintings in heaven, listen to my interview with her here: https://podcast.jordanraynor.com/episodes/joni-eareckson-tada-author-of-the-awesome-super-fantastic-forever-party.

said, the two roots that allow this lie to grow are the Abridged Gospel, which we addressed in chapter 1, and an incomplete understanding of the nature of eternity or heaven.

We need to address that second root here in chapter 2. N. T. Wright, whom *Christianity Today* has called "the most prolific biblical scholar in a generation,"[9] explains why:

> As long as we see salvation in terms of going to heaven when we die, the main work of the church is bound to be seen in terms of saving souls for that future. But when we see salvation, as the New Testament sees it, in terms of God's promised new heavens and new earth . . . then the main work of the church here and now demands to be rethought in consequence.[10]

The question, then, is, What does God's Word say about the nature of heaven? Many Christians have been given answers to that question that are only half-true. They're not full-blown lies, but they're incomplete enough to steal our joy, anticipation, and purpose in the present. As the "prince of preachers,"[11] Charles Spurgeon once said, "Discernment is not knowing the difference between right and wrong. It is knowing the difference between right and almost right."[12]

Until we grasp a more accurate and biblical picture of heaven, it will be impossible to see the full extent to which our work matters for eternity. So without further ado, let's replace five half truths about heaven with five whole truths together.

HALF TRUTH 1: HEAVEN IS A PLACE WE GO IN THE FUTURE

Just before he was martyred, "Stephen, full of the Holy Spirit, looked up to heaven and saw the glory of God, and Jesus standing at the right hand of God. 'Look,' he said, 'I see heaven open and the Son of Man standing at the right hand of God'" (Acts 7:55–56).

It's clear from this account that Stephen was glimpsing another physical realm. So it *is* true that heaven is a place. And it's *also* true that Christians enter that place in the future. Jesus demonstrated this when he looked at the criminal on the cross next to him and said, "Today you will be with me in paradise" (Luke 23:43).

But it's also clear that heaven is *much more* than just a place we go in the future. Jesus talked about the kingdom of heaven in the future *and* present tense saying that "the kingdom of heaven *has* come near" (Matthew 3:2) and "the kingdom of God *is* at hand" (Mark 1:15, ESV). By the way, those terms "kingdom of heaven" and "kingdom of God" are interchangeable. As many theologians have explained, " 'God's kingdom' and 'kingdom of heaven' mean the same thing."[13]

And the kingdom of God, the kingdom of heaven—whatever you want to call it—is more than just a physical place. Heaven is *also* a state of affairs.

See Matthew 10:7–8 as a case in point. Jesus said to his disciples, "Proclaim as you go, saying, 'The kingdom of heaven is at hand.' Heal the sick, raise the dead, cleanse lepers, cast out demons" (ESV). Clearly, Jesus wasn't referring to heaven as a physical place here. In this passage and others, Jesus used the word *heaven* to describe a changing world order.

So how can we define heaven? Dr. R. Paul Stevens defines it as not primarily "a realm [or] territory, but the rule of God as King"—"essentially the spread of the goodness and shalom of God in the world and in human life."[14] In *The Jesus Storybook Bible,* Sally Lloyd-Jones defines heaven as "wherever God is King."[15] But my favorite definition comes from Dallas Willard, who says that the kingdom of heaven is simply "where what God wants done is done."[16]

Those definitions help us replace our first half truth about heaven:

Half Truth 1: Heaven is a place we go in the future.

Whole Truth 1: Heaven is a place *and* a state of affairs, visible in part now *and* in full in the future.

That last part is critical. Because it's clear that our world isn't yet "where what God wants done is done," right? As we saw in chapter 1, the kingdom has been inaugurated but not yet fully implemented and consummated.* So we live today in what some call "the already and not yet" of the kingdom.[17] Dr. Sandra Richter explains this idea:

> With Jesus' entry into our world, the kingdom is *already* here. The new covenant has begun. God has invaded our exile, and every man, woman and child of Adam's race has been extended the invitation to come home. Death is defeated, Heaven is ours. Satan knows it is just a matter of time. Yet we still await the kingdom's consummation, the *not yet*.[18]

---

* This feels like an appropriate place to state that I have zero interest in getting into a debate about premillennialism, postmillennialism, etc. Why? Because, at the end of the day, these streams all end up flowing to the same destination: the eternal kingdom of heaven. In the words of Randy Alcorn, "Our beliefs about the Millennium need not affect our view of [heaven]," so I'm not going to waste your precious time debating the issue. Randy Alcorn, *Heaven* (Carol Stream, Ill.: Tyndale Momentum, 2004), 146. And now, back to our regularly scheduled programming.

In the meantime, we "citizens of heaven" work alongside Jesus the Gardener to close the gap between the *already* and the *not yet* (see Philippians 3:20). That's the whole point of "enter[ing] the kingdom of heaven" (Matthew 7:21)! As pastor John Ortberg puts it, "Salvation isn't about getting you into heaven; it's about getting heaven into you"—so that you can partner with Jesus to reveal more of heaven on earth.[19] And as we'll soon see, heaven contains far more than just God and his people.

HALF TRUTH 2: EARTH IS OUR TEMPORARY HOME

This half truth is peddled *everywhere* outside and inside the church today. Prominent pastors preach, "[Earth] is not your permanent home or final destination. You're just passing through, just visiting earth."[20] Funerals are laden with language about loved ones "going home to be with Jesus." And *American Idol* winners sing, "This is our temporary home. It's not where we belong."[21] (I love you, Carrie Underwood. I really do. Voted for you over Bo Bice and everything.)

Let's start with what's true about this half truth. The moment a Christian experiences physical death, their body stays here on earth and their "spirit [or soul] returns to God" (Ecclesiastes 12:7). So it's true that we Christians leave this earth and go to heaven when we die. The lie is that we *stay* there.

Unpacking one of Jesus's most famous quotes will help us understand this. In John 14:2, he said, "My Father's house has many rooms; if that were not so, would I have told you that I am going there to prepare a place for you?" But check this out: The Greek word Jesus used here for "rooms" is *monē,* which means "*temporary* lodging."[22]

Our "mansions in the sky" aren't permanent residences.[23] They're more like Airbnbs. Because ultimately it is not we who go to heaven, but heaven—and the souls of the redeemed currently in heaven—that comes to earth.

And it's worth mentioning that while many Christians today view heaven as their ultimate hope, *the first Christians never did*. The New Testament writers didn't focus on going to heaven when they died and spending eternity as disembodied spirits in a galaxy far, far away. Their ultimate hope was for physical, bodily resurrection—for "life *after* life after death."[24]

The apostle Paul says that he and his followers "groan inwardly as [they] wait eagerly." For what? Not going to heaven when they die! But "the redemption of [their] *bodies*" (Romans 8:23).

And where are those physical resurrected bodies going to live? On a physical resurrected *earth*. This is precisely what we see in Revelation 21:1–3. The apostle John writes,

> I saw "a new heaven and a new earth," for the first heaven and the first earth had passed away, and there was no longer any sea. I saw the Holy City, the new Jerusalem, coming down out of heaven from God, prepared as a bride beautifully dressed for her husband. And I heard a loud voice from the throne saying, "Look! God's dwelling place is now among the people, and he will dwell with them. They will be his people, and God himself will be with them and be their God."

Belinda Carlisle was right after all: Ultimately "heaven *is* a place on earth."[25] Contrary to what the homilies and hymns might teach you, God never intended to "fit us for heaven to live with [him] there."[26] He promised heaven on earth and to dwell with us *here*. Which is precisely what Jesus taught his followers to pray for! "Thy kingdom come. Thy will be done *on earth,* as it is in Heaven" (Matthew 6:10, KJ21).

But hang on, Jordan. I thought the Bible says the earth is going to be destroyed in the end. It's all going to burn up.

This common misconception is rooted in what pastor John Mark Comer calls a "borderline heretical" interpretation of 2 Peter 3:10[27] and, more specifically, the King James Version of that verse which reads like this: "The day of the Lord will come as a thief in the night; in the which the heavens shall pass away with a great noise, and the elements shall melt with fervent heat, the earth also and the works that are therein shall be burned up."

Sounds pretty clear that earth *is* our temporary home, right? Not so fast. Stick with me through this lengthy but helpful explanation from N. T. Wright:

> [In 2 Peter 3:10] we have a statement which in older translations of the Bible came out one way, but which, with all the biblical manuscripts we now have, almost certainly needs to be changed. In the older versions, this passage ends with the warning that "the earth and all the works on it *will be burned up.*" A cosmic destruction: the end of the physical world! Is that really what Peter wrote? If so, it's the only place in the whole of early Christian literature where such an idea is found.
>
> But in some manuscripts of the New Testament, including two of the very best, the word for "will be burned up" isn't there. Instead, there is a word which means "will be found," or "will be discovered," or "will be disclosed." Perhaps "will be found out" would be another way of getting at the meaning.[28]

And that makes perfect sense based on the context of 2 Peter 3. Peter is comparing the Day of the Lord to Noah and the Flood (see verse 6). And we all know that the Flood didn't *annihilate* the earth. It *purified* it, wiping out its imperfections so that the good stuff would be "discovered," "disclosed," and "found out."

So it will be at the end of this age. Jesus said so himself in Matthew 24:37: "As it was in the days of Noah, so it will be at the coming of the Son of Man."

Contrary to what fearmongering end-times propaganda might have you believe, God will use fire to purify the earth, not obliterate it. The earth won't be "vaporized like the Death Star" in *Star Wars*.[29] If you're looking for a pop-culture analogy for the New Earth, you'll find a much more accurate one in Disney's *Moana*.*

One of the main characters in *Moana* is a beautiful personified island named Te Fiti who is covered with lush green grass, towering trees, and the most vibrantly colored flowers you can imagine—probably a decent picture of what earth looked like prior to the Fall.

But when Te Fiti's heart is stolen, her beauty crumbles. Her once-gorgeous exterior is covered with lava rock, and Te Fiti turns into a monstrous version of her former self. Her appearance is *so* different that everyone mistakes her for an entirely different being.

But the movie doesn't end with Te Fiti being destroyed. It ends with her being renewed. When Moana restores the heart of Te Fiti, the island's hardened exterior begins to break, and the original Te Fiti—beautiful, lush, and colorful—emerges. The contrast is so stark that this appears to be a brand-new island. But of course, it's not. It's the original Te Fiti, but better. Not a new island, but one that is *like* new.[30]

That's the best picture I've ever seen of what Scripture

---

* I have to seriously discipline myself not to over-reference this rich film. What can I say? I can't resist the combination of the Rock and Lin-Manuel Miranda.

says will happen to the earth. In Revelation 21:5 (ESV), Jesus said, "Behold, I am making all things new"—*not* "I am making all new things." And that applies to the work he will do to the earth.* Our hope is not for a whole *new* world but for a whole *renewed* world. And that renewed world—that purified, physical, material earth—will be the final resting place of heaven.

Which, of course, makes perfect sense given the context of the Unabridged Gospel. In act 1, God deemed all the world—not just human beings—good (see Genesis 1). And in act 3, Jesus came "to reconcile to himself *all things*" (Colossians 1:20). And "all things" includes the earth! God "is not a Creator who rejects and replaces; he reconciles and redeems."[31]

Okay, let's break this down really explicitly to make sure we're all on the same page. We can think of heaven in two stages: the Present Heaven and the Eternal Heaven on Earth. If you're a Christian, the Present Heaven is where your soul will go if, God forbid, you get hit by a bus today.

But one day God will make the Present Heaven fully visible on a New Earth, where heaven and earth will be married forever, creating the Eternal Heaven on Earth, where he will dwell with us for ever and ever (see Revelation 21:1–5). Which brings us to our second whole truth:

Half Truth 2: Earth is our temporary home.

Whole Truth 2: Earth is our temporary home *until* it is our permanent home.

---

* Fun fact: The word we translate as "new" in "new earth" in Revelation 21:1 is *kainos,* which can be translated as "new" *or* "renewed." John Mark Comer, *Garden City: Work, Rest, and the Art of Being Human* (Grand Rapids, Mich.: Zondervan, 2015), 249. I know. I have a loose, nerdy definition of *fun.*

In just a second, I'm going to spell out exactly what this means for your work today. But first I want to look you in the eye, reader, because I know some of you are sitting there thinking, *Jordan, I've spent my whole life in the church. How have I never heard this?*

I used to wonder the same thing. I went to a Christian school for thirteen years and never *ever* heard this.* I sincerely believed that earth was my temporary home and that we're all "just a-passing through."[32] If you've fallen for the same lie, *please* hear this: In all likelihood, *it's not your fault.* Please don't blame yourself.

You and a few generations of Christians have been victims of theological malpractice. Not malice—just carelessness (or perhaps ignorance), because many churches today simply never preach these truths! As theologian Darrell Cosden lamented nearly twenty years ago, "The belief that our ultimate salvation hope is the bodily resurrection to a transformed and genuinely physical new heaven and new earth has been relegated to the spiritual background, in danger of being lost altogether."[33]

What has replaced a *biblical* theology of heaven is what one author calls "lifeboat theology," which leads many Christians to act "as if the creation were the *Titanic,* and now that we've hit the iceberg of sin, there's nothing left for us to do but get ourselves into lifeboats. The ship is sinking rapidly, God has given up on it and is concerned only with the survival of his people."[34] And any effort you or I make to produce a movie, scale a business, or make a bottle of wine is the equivalent of "rearranging the deck chairs" on the sinking ship.[35]

---

* To be fair, maybe I did and I simply wasn't paying attention.

But everything we've seen thus far totally debunks that lie! As Fleming Rutledge once said, "The church is not a redeemed boat floating in an unredeemed sea."[36]

Why does this matter? Because "the significance of secular work depends on the value of creation, and the value of creation depends on its final destiny."[37] And because God values his creation enough to save it, our creations must also have intrinsic value to God. In the words of Randy Alcorn,

> When we think of Heaven as unearthly, our present lives seem unspiritual, like they don't matter. When we grasp the reality of the New Earth, our present, earthly lives suddenly matter. Conversations with loved ones matter. The taste of food matters. Work, leisure, creativity, and intellectual stimulation matter. Rivers and trees and flowers matter. Laughter matters. Service matters. Why? *Because they are eternal.*[38]

That brings us to our ninth proposition about how our work has eternal value beyond leveraging it to the instrumental end of sharing the gospel with our co-workers:

Proposition 9: Your work has intrinsic value because God promises to carry the material world into eternity.

And because God promises to save the material world and not just the spiritual realm of souls, the work you and I do following the First Commission—making the material world more useful, more beautiful, more functional, and more true to God's original design—has eternal value. If that comes as a surprise to you, then the next whole truth is going to blow your mind.

HALF TRUTH 3: WE ARE GOING BACK TO EDEN

In my experience, even those who understand that heaven is ultimately here on earth have an anemic vision of what all that actually entails. Their views of the New Earth are marked by a "vague and wishy-washy piety" that is more shaped by culture than by Scripture.[39]

One of those views is that the New Earth will be merely a return to the Garden of Eden. As with each of the other half truths in this chapter, this one contains a modicum of validity. In Revelation 21 and 22, we see that everything sin broke in Eden in Genesis 3 has been renewed and that "the tree of life" is once again at the center of the earth, its leaves used for "the healing of the nations" (22:2).

But the *location* of the tree of life is the first clue that the Eternal Heaven on Earth is much more than just Eden 2.0. In Revelation 22:1–2, John says, "The angel showed me the river of the water of life, as clear as crystal, flowing from the throne of God and of the Lamb down the middle of the great street of the city. On each side of the river stood the tree of life."*

So, unlike the Eden we know from Genesis 1, this vision is of the garden *surrounded by a city*. The picture of our eternal dwelling place isn't us living in nature's paradise out in the boonies. It's more like Central Park in New York City— a beautiful natural paradise encased by excellent works of culture.

But even though many believe that New York is the greatest city in the world today, it doesn't hold a candle to the city

---

* I've always said that world-class cities require water. This is biblical exhibit A. Love you, Tampa Bay.

the Garden of Eden will eventually call home. This is the inimitable City of God—"the Holy City, the new Jerusalem" (Revelation 21:2). And John's description of the city is *mindboggling.*

He says that the New Jerusalem is a cubed city measuring "12,000 stadia in length, and as wide and high as it is long" (verse 16). For those of you who haven't brushed up on your first-century forms of measurement, "12,000 stadia" is roughly 1,400 miles. Yes, you read that right: The New Jerusalem stands 1,400 *miles* tall, deep, and wide.

If this were a city in the United States, its base would extend from Canada in the north to Mexico in the south and from Los Angeles in the west to Dallas in the east. That's nearly two million square miles, or roughly forty times the size of England, seven times the size of Texas, or four times the size of Colombia.* And remember, *that's just the ground floor!*

But it's not just the size of the New Jerusalem that's impressive. It's also the city's extravagant beauty. Remember the gold, pearls, and onyx Adam and Eve were meant to unearth back in Genesis 2? They have now been used to create golden streets, pearly gates, and foundations "decorated with every kind of precious stone" (see Revelation 21:18–21).

In case you couldn't tell from John's description, this city is *not* the work of human hands. It's the work of God alone— the Master Craftsman (see Hebrews 11:10).†

The very presence of this city in the Eternal Heaven on Earth reiterates a truth we saw in chapter 1—namely, that

---

* Sorry, Texas friends. I couldn't resist putting "everything's bigger in Texas" in its proper context.

† A little nod to one of the only novels I've ever enjoyed: *The Master Craftsman* by my good friend Kelli Stuart.

God values people *and* culture, so much so that right now he is at work designing and constructing a city for us to dwell in together. And he promises to carry his magnum opus—the work of his hands—into eternity.

If that's surprising to you, then this is going to knock your socks off: It's not just the work of God's hands that will be physically present in the Eternal Heaven on Earth. It's some of the work of *human* hands as well.

After describing the New Jerusalem, John says this in Revelation 21:25–26: "On no day will its gates ever be shut, for there will be no night there. The glory and honor of the nations will be brought into [the city]."

"The glory and honor of the nations." What is John talking about? Thankfully, we don't have to guess, because Isaiah answered that question for us in the Old Testament. And even though Isaiah wrote some eight hundred years before John, scholars agree that "both men were working with the same material."[40] So "Isaiah 60 serves as the best biblical commentary on Revelation 21–22."[41]

In that commentary, Isaiah says this: "Your gates will always stand open . . . so that people may bring you the wealth of the nations" (verse 11). This language is nearly identical to John's. But Isaiah lists out what some of "the wealth of the nations" is.

It includes the ships of Tarshish (see verse 9), incense from the nation of Sheba (see verse 6), and refined silver and gold from some unnamed nation (see verse 9). Make no mistake about it: Ships, incense, refined silver and gold—these are all *works of human hands.* And Isaiah and John are watching Jesus welcome these cultural goods into the New Jerusalem.

The implication here is startling. These prophetic visions suggest that some of the work of your hands—the product you're building, the book you're writing, the truck you're repairing—has the chance of literally, *physically* lasting into eternity.

And again, this makes perfect sense given the context of the Unabridged Gospel! (Aren't you glad you trudged through chapter 1?) Because as Dr. Richard Mouw explains, "There is an important sense in which the Holy City is the Garden-plus-the-'filling'"[42] that God called us to create in the First Commission—redeemed, purified, and laid at the feet of Jesus as an act of worship.

Cosden says, "One might have thought that the pre-Fall Garden of Eden, what God created alone, would have been a more fitting image [for heaven]. Although many Christians have thought that heaven is simply a return to Eden, this is not the case in [John's] vision."[43] The New Jerusalem will "include what we have accomplished through work. For what we have done, our 'splendor,' will be brought and put on display as part of the 'glory and honor of the nations'."[44]

That brings us to our third whole truth about heaven:

Half Truth 3: We are going back to Eden.

Whole Truth 3: We are going back to Eden *surrounded by* the work of God's hands and some of our own.

Now, I know this might still sound unbelievable to you. So let me quickly spell out three reasons (beyond the passages of Scripture we've just read) why we can take this idea to the bank.

First, *it's simply not in God's nature to ask his children to create things only to destroy them.*

Imagine for a second that I asked my kids to paint me a picture and, after they joyfully brought it to me, I threw it in the trash. That would be monstrously cruel, right? But to say that all our work is going to burn up in the end is to accuse God of this cruelty. Because the very first thing God asked us to do—the First Commission to humankind—was to take the raw materials of creation and to make more with them.

It's simply not in God's character to watch his children obey that command by making paintings, software, and Nutella only to throw those creations away. Good earthly fathers don't do that. Do we really think our perfect heavenly Father will? In the words of the Little Mermaid, "I don't see how a world that makes such wonderful things could be bad."[45] Or the things themselves.

Second, *kingdoms have more than just people and kings.*

Jesus could have described eternity as merely a return to Eden, but he didn't. He consistently described it as a kingdom. And while that kingdom will be marked by the intangible values of justice, peace, and love, it will also be marked by tangible things such as telescopes, books, and—*please* let me be right about this—Chick-fil-A.

Finally, *by redeeming the work of our hands, God will get greater glory.*

I want to make this crystal clear lest anyone misinterpret me: *Jesus is the ultimate treasure of heaven!* John Piper is right in saying that "people who would be happy in heaven if Christ were not there, will not be there."[46] But that truth need not lead us to a false piety that replaces the hope of our work literally lasting forever with guilt and shame. Because when Christ redeems the work of our hands, he will get even greater glory. Randy Alcorn *nails* this saying:

> Some may think it silly or sentimental to suppose that nature, animals, paintings, books, or a baseball bat might be resurrected. It may appear to trivialize the coming resurrection. I would suggest that it does ex-

actly the opposite: It *elevates* resurrection, emphasizing the power of Christ to radically renew mankind—and far more. God promises to resurrect not only humanity but also the creation that fell as a result of our sin. Because God will resurrect the earth itself, we know that the resurrection of the dead extends to things that are inanimate. Even some of the works of our hands, done to God's glory, will survive.[47]

If this still sounds too good to be true, stick with me until chapter 4, where we'll do a deeper dive into what work we can expect to last into the Eternal Heaven on Earth. For now, I want you to see how everything we just saw helps us debunk the lie that the only way our work matters for eternity is if we leverage it to the instrumental end of saving souls. Here's our next proposition:

Proposition 10: Your work has intrinsic value because God will carry the work of his hands and some of our own into eternity.

You see, if we want to be "theologically consistent, we as Christians should value most highly whatever God values (as determined by what he will save)."[48] And we've just seen that God will save far more than human souls! He will save at least some of the work of human hands. That means that your work beyond evangelism—your work making skyscrapers, art, and software—must have intrinsic and eternal value to God. Andy Crouch puts it this way:

Knowing that the new Jerusalem will be furnished with the best of every culture frees us from having to give a "religious" or evangelistic explanation for everything we do. We are free to simply make the best we can of the world, in concert with our forebears and our neighbors. If the ships of Tarshish and the camels of Midian can find a place in the new Jerusalem, our work, no matter how "secular," can too.[49]

HALF TRUTH 4: WE WILL WORSHIP FOR ETERNITY

Okay, so heaven is ultimately on earth, and it contains far more than just God and his people. But what on earth will we be *doing* on earth for all eternity? John Eldredge says, "This is probably the one aspect of our future most shrouded in religious vapors, fogged in by a pea soup of vagueness, emptiness, and heavenly foam."[50] I couldn't agree more.

If Hollywood is to be believed, heaven will be a tearfully boring place. See the TV comedy *The Good Place* as a case in point. The show follows the lives of its characters in heaven, which is all fun and games for a while. But (spoiler alert) the characters become so bored that they essentially commit suicide, choosing to become "energy dust" rather than remain in the Good Place.[51]

Those characters would have shouted a hearty amen to Isaac Asimov's remark that "whatever the tortures of hell, I think the boredom of heaven would be even worse."[52]

While I never said those words out loud, I quietly agreed with that statement for a long, *long* time. I remember sitting in chapel in elementary school, horrified at the idea of spending billions of years playing a harp. The idea of heaven wasn't a source of hope for me. It was a source of dread.

Over the years, I've heard *many* adults and kids admit those same fears in hushed whispers laden with shame, which is why I'm convinced that one of Satan's favorite tactics for discouraging God's people is to make heaven look dreadfully boring. The Enemy doesn't need to convince us that heaven isn't real. He just needs to convince us that heaven is lame. Because if he can do that, he can steal our joy, hope, and obedience. He can make it impossible to justify the cost of the fight.

This idea that heaven is a bore is rooted in the half truth that we will be worshipping for all eternity. Now, Scripture does make clear that we will worship God forever, but the reason I call this a *half* truth is that our understanding of the word *worship* is, at best, half-true.

When we think of worship, we think almost exclusively of *musical* worship. And while there will certainly be musical worship in the Eternal Heaven on Earth (see Isaiah 51:11), God's definition of worship is much broader than strumming a harp or lyre. A quick trip back to act 1 of the Unabridged Gospel will help make this clear.

Genesis 2:15 says that "God took the man and put him in the Garden of Eden to work it and take care of it." The word we translate as "work" in this verse is the Hebrew word *abad,* which is the exact same word we translate as "worship" in Exodus 3:12.

That means that Adam and Eve were worshipping God *not just* when they walked with him in the garden or sang him a song. They were worshipping God as they carried out the First Commission to fill, subdue, and rule the earth on his behalf. And in what may come as the greatest shock of this book so far, *the same will be true for you and me for all eternity.* Revelation 22:3–5 makes this crystal clear:

> No longer will there be any curse. The throne of God and of the Lamb will be in the city, and his servants will serve him. They will see his face, and his name will be on their foreheads. There will be no more night. They

will not need the light of a lamp or the light of the sun,
for the Lord God will give them light. And they will
reign for ever and ever.

Did you catch that? God's Word doesn't say that we will
sing "Lord, I Lift Your Name on High" for ever and ever. Or
recline in a hammock for ever and ever. We will *reign* for ever
and ever. Which is precisely what God intended for us to do
from the very beginning.

You see it, right? Here in the final chapter of Scripture, we
see the exact same commission humankind was given in the
first chapter of Scripture. In Genesis 1, God created the world,
but he didn't finish it. He invited his image-bearers to fill,
subdue, and rule this world on his behalf. And here in Revelation 22, God is restoring our reign and once again delegating
his royal authority to you and me.

There's a stunning picture of this at the end of *The Lion,
the Witch and the Wardrobe*. Aslan, the Christlike lion, is clearly
capable of ruling Narnia all on his own. But instead, he shares
his authority with his subjects: "Aslan solemnly crowned
them and led them to the four thrones amid deafening shouts
of, 'Long Live King Peter! Long Live Queen Susan! Long
Live King Edmund! Long Live Queen Lucy!'"[53] And then the
great lion turns to his deputies and says, "Once a king or
queen in Narnia, *always* a king or queen."[54]

If I were forced to summarize the mission of humankind
in a single line from a novel, that would be it. Because as
we've seen, the story of Scripture is that we were made to be
royals but we sinned, abdicating our thrones. But—praise
God—Christ came to save our lives *and* to restore us to our
original purpose: ruling the world with him and for him, a
reign that starts now and lasts for evermore.

But what exactly does it mean that we "will reign for ever

and ever" with Christ? It means that we will *work* for ever and ever with Christ. As much as it pains me to call out the great songwriter Vince Gill, "your work on earth" is *not* done after you die.[55] Because just as the paradise of Eden was a *vocation* and not a *vacation,* so it will be in the Eternal Heaven on Earth.

And for the first time in millennia, human work will be perfect and painless once again. God said this explicitly in one of the most hopeful passages in all of Scripture:

> See, I will create
>   new heavens and a new earth. . . .
> [My people] will build houses and dwell in them;
>   they will plant vineyards and eat their fruit.
> No longer will they build houses and others live in them,
>   or plant and others eat.
> For as the days of a tree,
>   so will be the days of my people;
> my chosen ones will long enjoy
>   the work of their hands.
> They will not labor in vain. (Isaiah 65:17, 21–23)

What a vision! If you love your job, this promise should make you ecstatic about the Eternal Heaven on Earth. And if you hate your job, this promise should give you great hope. Because a day is coming when every single one of God's "chosen ones will long *enjoy* the work of their hands." This is work as it was always meant to be without the "thorns and thistles" of the curse (Genesis 3:18). It's work that is challenging but satisfying. Difficult but fruitful. All honey, no stings.

I don't know about you, but that sounds *way* more exciting than endless harpsichords and hammocks. But you may be wondering, *What specific work will I be doing for eternity?* Let me offer three guesses based on clues we find throughout God's Word.

First, *we may do the same work we're doing in this life, with all of the best parts and none of the bad.*

Revelation 14:13 says, "Blessed are the dead who die in the Lord from now on . . . for their deeds will follow them." And the word translated as "deeds" here is that Greek word *ergon,* which (as we saw in chapter 1) denotes "work, task, employment."[56] John Mark Comer translates it as "occupation."[57]

This seems to imply that some of our current occupations will follow us into eternity. Now, clearly some jobs will be irrelevant in the Eternal Heaven on Earth. Nurses, soldiers, and counselors are going to have to find new gigs. But podcasters, scientists, and painters like Joni Eareckson Tada may very well continue to hone their crafts as acts of worship for all eternity.

Second, *we may finish the work we leave unfinished in this life.*

There's a quote from theologian Karl Rahner that I think about a lot: "In the torment of the insufficiency of everything attainable, we learn that ultimately in this world there is no finished symphony."[58]

That's what so many of us dread, isn't it? Leaving our life's work unfinished? As Jim Croce laments, "There never seems to be enough time to do the things you want to do once you find them."[59] But because the New Testament promises continuity between this life and the next—for our bodies, the earth, and even some of the work of our hands—it stands to reason that we will have the chance to continue working on some of the "symphonies" we left unfinished in this life.

One of the founders of Fuller Theological Seminary agrees, saying that "we will be permitted to finish many of those worthy tasks which we had dreamed to do while on earth but which neither time nor strength nor ability allowed us to achieve."[60]

Finally, in the Eternal Heaven on Earth, *we may do the work we wanted to do in this life but couldn't.*

One of my best friends is a *crazy* talented screenwriter. When he writes, he feels God's pleasure.[61] But for whatever reason, he's never caught his big break. So he goes to work every day in a corporate job that he's very thankful for, but it isn't really *him.*

My friend might never turn one of his scripts into a film in this life. But I think he will in the next one. Not just for his pleasure, but primarily for God's greater glory. Because it's partly through excellent work that we "proclaim the excellencies" of Christ (1 Peter 2:9, ESV).

Ephesians 2:10 says there are "good works . . . God prepared in advance for us to do." We've already seen what those good works are generally (filling, subduing, and ruling the world for God's glory). But it's also clear that there are specific works God designed each of us to do best. Work we feel he *made* us to do.

But the curse makes it difficult, and oftentimes impossible, to do that work in this life. Maybe God made you to be an astronaut, but you were born in a time and place that made that impossible. Or maybe you were once a great writer, but life happened, and you've spent decades ignoring the craft you love so that you can pay the bills.

If that's you, take heart: It's perfectly in line with God's character to give his people "the desires of [their] heart," *including* their desires for their work (Psalm 37:4). As one biblical scholar puts it, "The work on the other side, whatever be its character, will be adapted to each one's special aptitude and powers. It will be the work he can do best; the work that will give the fullest play to all that is within him."[62]

Professor Dumbledore was right: "To the well-organized mind, death is but the next great adventure."[63] Here's how I summed up Scripture's vision of eternal worship in my children's book *The Royal in You:*

> So don't think for one second that heaven is boring,
> because we'll be reigning, creating, and exploring!
> Not just for our joy, and surely not for our glory,
> but to love and to worship the One who is worthy.
> It'll be so much better than your wildest dreams—
> ruling heaven on earth next to Jesus our King.

All of this brings us to our fourth whole truth about heaven:

Half Truth 4: We will worship for eternity.

Whole Truth 4: We will worship for eternity *by* singing *and* by filling, subduing, and ruling the Eternal Heaven on Earth with King Jesus.

And that truth gives us even more reason to believe that our work today has intrinsic value to God. Here's our next proposition:

Proposition 11: Your work has intrinsic value because it's what God created you to do for eternity.

If we will be filling, subduing, and ruling over creation with Christ forever, then the work you do with him today as a manager, zookeeper, or designer is anything but temporal. You are rehearsing for eternity. And so, you are free to lean into your work with God and for him today, knowing that the First Commission is the only one that will never end.

Here's our final half truth about heaven.

HALF TRUTH 5: WE ARE CALLED TO KEEP WATCH FOR CHRIST'S RETURN

As we saw at the beginning of this chapter, you and I live in the *already* and *not yet* of the kingdom of heaven. The kingdom has been inaugurated, but we are still waiting for God to completely and permanently rip the veil between heaven and earth and consummate the marriage between these two dimensions (see Revelation 21).

While we wait, we are called to look out for the second coming of Christ. Jesus said this explicitly in Matthew 25:13: "Keep watch, because you do not know the day or the hour." The reason it's only *half*-true that you and I are called to wait for the consummation of heaven and earth is found in our interpretation of Jesus's call to "keep watch."

Many of us have been taught to interpret this to mean a passive sort of watching marked by endless study and speculation about when and where Christ will return. This largely American infatuation with the second coming of Christ has become the preferred source of infotainment for many. Which is sad because this is *not even close* to the kind of watching Jesus called us to.

Immediately after he instructed his disciples to "keep watch," Jesus launched into his famous parable of the talents, the story of a master (representing Jesus) who puts his servants to work while they wait for his return (see Matthew 25:14–30). Jesus couldn't have made it any clearer: We are called to keep watch for his return not by *sitting* on our hands but by *working* with them.

This truth is reiterated throughout Paul's letters, perhaps most notably in 1 Corinthians 15. That chapter is Paul's longest exposition on the Christian hope of bodily resurrection in the Eternal Heaven on Earth. As he comes to the end of his writing on this topic, he doesn't say, "Okay, guys, knowing that heaven is coming, sit back and wait, because ultimately nothing you do in this life matters." In fact, he says the exact *opposite*.

In verse 58, Paul says, "Therefore, my dear brothers and sisters, stand firm. Let nothing move you. Always give yourselves fully to the work of the Lord, because you know that your labor in the Lord is not in vain."

Paul is saying that, in light of the glorious promises about heaven that we've explored in this chapter, we aren't called just to wait. We are called to work in anticipation of the day in which God's dimension of heaven covers the face of the New Earth. That brings us to our fifth and final whole truth about heaven:

Half Truth 5: We are called to keep watch for Christ's return.

Whole Truth 5: We are called to keep watch for Christ's return *by* giving ourselves fully to the work of the Lord.

And it's that "work of the Lord" that Paul says "is not in vain." Another translation renders those words as "the work you're doing will not be worthless."[64] Paul is saying that somehow, mind-blowing as it may seem, the work you and I do in the present will shape eternity.

And we can be *certain* that "the work of the Lord" means much more than just the "spiritual" tasks of evangelism and prayer for at least three reasons.

First, *Paul's main aim in 1 Corinthians 15 appears to be tearing down the false divide between the spiritual and material realms.**

Second, *the work of the Lord, Jesus Christ, was far more than just evangelism,* as we saw in chapter 1.

Finally, *all sorts of work can be done "in the Lord"* (1 Corinthians 15:58). What does the phrase "labor in the Lord" mean? One leading New Testament scholar says it means *anything* "we do in Christ and by the Spirit."[65] Pastor Bruce Milne renders it as "*everything,* literally, which flows out of our faith-relationship with the Ever-Living One."[66] The New Living Translation translates Paul's words to mean *any* work "you do for the Lord."

In sum, any work you do for *your* fame, for *your* fortune, and according to *your* rules will perish. But any work you do for *God's* glory, powered by *God's* Spirit, and according to *God's* rules will last forever. N. T. Wright summarizes this beautifully:

> You are not oiling the wheels of a machine that's about to roll over a cliff. You are not restoring a great painting that's shortly going to be thrown on the fire. You are not planting roses in a garden that's about to be dug up for a building site. You are—strange though it may seem, almost as hard to believe as the resurrection itself—accomplishing something that will become in due course part of God's new world.[67]

---

* As Dr. Darrell Cosden explains, "Although some might be inclined to see 'labor in the Lord' or the Lord's work only as what we traditionally call 'spiritual' ministry, nothing in the text necessarily limits our participation in and witness to the resurrection to narrowly 'religious' working activity. Indeed, getting away from a narrow view of what is 'spiritual' that downplays physical life seems to be the whole point of Paul's teaching on the physical resurrection." Darrell Cosden, *The Heavenly Good of Earthly Work* (Milton Keynes, U.K.: Paternoster, 2006), 62.

In part 1 of this book, we've been confronting the pervasive, unbiblical lie that the only work of eternal consequence is work that is leveraged to the *instrumental* end of carrying out the Great Commission. As we've hacked away at the roots of that lie (an abridged understanding of the gospel and these five half truths about heaven), I've laid out a series of propositions about why your work has *intrinsic* value to God. Here's the last of those propositions:

> **Proposition 12:** Your work has intrinsic value because God promises that any work done "in the Lord is not in vain."

Now we're finally ready to answer the big question: How exactly is our work "not in vain"? In what specific ways do our jobs shape eternity?

In part 2 of this book, I'll share the four answers to that question that have been most life-changing for me. And while this is far from an exhaustive list of how our work matters for eternity, I'm confident that these four ways will lead you to unparalleled hope and faithfulness in the present.

YOUR SACRED RESPONSE

I love making detailed plans for vacations, partly because I'm a type A control freak but also because planning gets me excited for my trips. Sadly, most of us spend more time planning a vacation than we do planning for eternity.[68] Let's begin to fix that with this simple but powerful practice.

Now that you've replaced half truths about heaven with the whole truths you explored in this chapter, I want you to use your biblically informed imagination to list out the first three things you want to do in the Eternal Heaven on Earth.

You'll find space to write this list in *The Sacred Response* workbook, which you can download for free at jordanraynor.com/response. There you'll also find Joni Eareckson Tada's incredible response to this prompt along with an additional practice to help you articulate where you see yourself professionally in five million years.

PART II

Four Ways Your Job Matters for Eternity

HOW TO CONTRIBUTE TO GOD'S ETERNAL PLEASURE EVEN IF YOU'RE NOT CHANGING THE WORLD

Chassie Anders was born to be a hairstylist. "I kind of struggled in school growing up," she shares, "but when I walked into cosmetology school, everything just made sense to me. . . . I was really good with my hands."[1] And quickly, Anders "fell in love" with her craft.[2]

But when she fell in love with Jesus Christ a few years later, she was surprised to find her local church pressuring her to give up her vocational gifts. The dominant message Anders heard from leaders in her church was that the Great Commission is the only commission for those who are serious about following Christ.

So, Anders says, "people didn't really take my work seriously."[3] She and her husband were told implicitly and explicitly that "what it means to be a Christ follower"[4] was to "quit our jobs, sell most of our belongings, and say goodbye to our life as we knew it" in Texas.[5] And while she was deeply passionate about following Jesus, overseas missions just didn't seem right for *her.*

"I feel like my church put a ministry goal of sending a certain number of people to the nations (an amazing thing, obviously) in front of me as an individual child of God," she explains in retrospect. "I don't think anyone was asking, how is Chassie wired, and how can she specifically make a difference in the world?"[6] It seemed like "my freedom to choose my calling, my freedom to choose how I specifically, uniquely follow Christ, was kind of taken from me in a way."[7]

So Anders and her husband followed the only path they knew to serve the Lord: signing a two-year agreement to serve as "full-time missionaries" in Asia. "In the Christian world, beauty and the types of things I love can be seen as vain," she explains. "So I figured it was the right choice to leave it behind."[8]

But it turned out that it *wasn't* the right choice for Anders and her husband. Asia was "extremely difficult for me personally," she says.[9] "I was *majorly* depressed."[10] And "even though I have a huge heart for missions and sharing the gospel . . . I felt so trapped."[11]

As they neared the end of their two-year commitment, the couple had an opportunity to leave Asia. On the one hand, it was an easy decision to go back home to Texas to serve God there. But Anders "felt immense guilt for wanting to leave and pressure to stay."[12]

In the end, the couple made the brave decision to follow God's call back to Texas. But Anders's guilt followed her home.

"I really struggled with going back to my work as a hairstylist," she says. "I believed the lies that my job was not good enough in the eyes of God and that beauty is so vain compared to sharing the gospel with the unreached. It made me question everything: being a Christian, my purpose, my worldview, church, especially my work."[13]

But it was the work itself that God used to begin to heal Anders's soul. "One of the things my husband would tell me during our first year back home was how happy I seemed after doing a styled shoot or working with a bride," she shares. "It was one of the few things that made my spirit feel . . . alive!"[14]

Over time, as Anders has meditated on many of the truths we covered in part 1 of this book, she has come to embrace her work as a hairstylist as just as legitimate a ministry as the work she did in Asia. What she once viewed as vain, she fervently declares is *not* in vain in God's eyes: "It's kingdom work," she says.[15]

How so? For starters, she leverages her work to the *instrumental* end of carrying out the Great Commission. "We get to share God's heart with our clients all the time," she says, and "give 10% of our profits" to missions.[16]

But Anders, like you, now sees the *intrinsic* value of her work as well: "My work *within itself* can be a means of reflecting redemption—reflecting God's original intent. Even the work of styling hair can bring God eternal pleasure."[17]

THE SMILE OF GOD IS THE GOAL OF YOUR LIFE

In part 1, we saw that our work has intrinsic, eternal value even when we aren't leveraging our jobs to the instrumental end of evangelism. That truth allowed us to dismantle the unbiblical hierarchy that elevates the work of pastors and other religious professionals above the work most of us mere Christians do as small-business owners, firefighters, or social workers.

But if we're not careful, another hierarchy can slip into our thinking: We can end up elevating the work of Christians most clearly "changing the world" above the work of those of us who are simply sustaining and serving it. Prosecuting human traffickers matters, but not selling insurance. Curing disease matters, but not waiting tables. Teaching kids matters, but not styling hair. I mean, come on. Can the work of a cosmetologist *really* "bring God eternal pleasure" when the world is going to hell in a handbasket?

Given our culture's obsession with utility and function, our first instinct may be to say no. As Makoto Fujimura has pointed out, the modern church "has been undermined by the utilitarian mindset of the Industrial Revolution. We see our existence and value only in terms of 'fixing the world.'"[18]

But that's not how God sees. All throughout Scripture, God shows that he values work beyond its usefulness. Genesis 2:9 says that he made "trees that were pleasing to the eye and good for food." There was no *need* for these trees to be "pleasing to the eye." But God values function *and* beauty so much that he called out the beauty of the trees *before* their usefulness!

We see the same principle at the opposite bookend of Scripture, where John describes the foundations of the New Jerusalem as being "decorated with every kind of precious stone" (Revelation 21:19). That's *5,600 miles* of emeralds, rubies, and other gems (see verses 19–20).

What purpose does 5,600 miles of ever-lovely jewels serve? My guess is none—and that's precisely the point! Because as theologian Gustavo Gutiérrez puts it, "Utility is not the primary reason for God's action."[19]

God doesn't limit his work to the useful and functional. He doesn't spend his time only fixing what's broken in the world. Sometimes he works just to bring himself glory and pleasure. And in the gospel of John, we see Jesus encouraging his followers to do the same:

> Mary took about a pint of . . . expensive perfume; she poured it on Jesus' feet and wiped his feet with her hair. And the house was filled with the fragrance of the perfume.
>
> But one of his disciples, Judas Iscariot . . . objected, "Why wasn't this perfume sold and the money given to the poor? It was worth a year's wages." (John 12:3–5)

Judas, like so many of us today, was obsessed with purpose and function. "How impractical!" we can hear him crying. But check out Jesus's response: "Leave her alone," he told Judas (John 12:7). Because what Mary did brought a smile to Jesus's face. And that was enough. Because, at the end of the day, "the smile of God is the goal of your life."[20]

In the introduction of this book, I promised to show you four ways your work matters for eternity. Here's the first:

Way 1: Your work matters for eternity because it is a vehicle for bringing God eternal pleasure.

Jesus's interaction with Mary shows us that the simplest, most foundational way our work matters for eternity is that it can be a vehicle for bringing an eternal smile to God's face. And that is enough because this is the essence of worship.

Now, *worship* is one of those churchy words that are used so much that nobody can agree on their meaning anymore. I've read *dozens* of definitions of *worship*. But my favorite, by far, comes from pastor Rick Warren, who says that worship is simply "bringing pleasure to God."[21]

You may have heard your pastor say that "all of life is worship"[22] or "work is worship"[23] and sat there scratching your head. *How in the world is sending an email, cleaning a pool, or writing a line of code worship?*

But if we define *worship* as "bringing pleasure to God," it starts to make a whole lot more sense, because Scripture says we can bring God pleasure in nearly *anything* we do. Psalm 37:23 says, "The LORD directs the steps of the godly. He delights in every detail of their lives" (NLT).

Did you catch that? God doesn't just delight in watching you give money to the poor, share the gospel, or fight for justice. He also delights in watching you design a website, build a home, or close a deal. "He delights in *every detail*" of the lives of the godly.

Clearly, God doesn't *need* us to bring him pleasure (see Acts 17:24–25). But in his graciousness, he allows for every detail of our lives to be an ingredient to his happiness. And his pleasure is eternal. Psalm 30:5 says, "His favor is for life" (NKJV)—both this life *and* the life to come, because Scripture promises that God will remember everything we ever do that brings him joy (see Hebrews 6:10).

The question, then, is, How can we work in ways that contribute to God's eternal happiness? Here are five answers to that question.

HOW TO BRING GOD ETERNAL PLEASURE

1. Obey His Commands

The first time the Gospels mention Jesus as an adult is at his baptism. After John plunged him into the water, Jesus heard his Father shout from the heavens: "You are my Son, whom I love; with you I am well pleased" (Luke 3:22).

Now, we know only two things about Jesus's life between the ages of twelve and thirty, when this baptism took place. We know that he worked as a carpenter or builder (see Mark 6:3) and that he was obedient to his parents and to God (see Luke 2:51). So what was the Father "well pleased" with in the life of Jesus? Apparently his simple, everyday obedience.

You and I can bring God pleasure in the same way today. In 1 John 3:22 it says that "we keep his commands and give him pleasure when he sees what we are doing" (NTE). That means when you simply "let your 'Yes' be 'Yes'" and do what you say you're going to do at work (Matthew 5:37, NKJV), when you "do good" to your enemies and competitors "without expecting to get anything back" (Luke 6:35), when you acknowledge Christ "before others" you work with (Matthew 10:32), when you "give thanks in all circumstances" (1 Thessalonians 5:18), and when you "pray . . . in secret" at your desk (Matthew 6:6)—*all* of that obedience brings eternal pleasure to God.

I could go on and on, but let's move on to see a few other ways we can bring God joy while we work.

2. Pursue the Ministry of Excellence

In 1957, God grabbed hold of the heart of John Coltrane, the great jazz saxophonist. What was Coltrane's response? To record an album as "a humble offering to Him."[24] But this wouldn't be just any old album. Motivated by his newfound faith, Coltrane was intent on reaching the pinnacle of his craft. And that he did, recording the now-legendary record *A Love Supreme.*

"One night, after an exceptionally brilliant performance" of the piece, Coltrane "stepped down from the stage and was heard to say, '*Nunc dimittis*'"—the same words Simeon uttered after holding the newborn Messiah (see Luke 2:25–32).[25] They essentially mean "I could die happy now."[26]

Why could Coltrane die happy? Because he knew he had performed so exceptionally well that he brought great pleasure to others. And that brought great pleasure to God.

In his letter to the Colossians, the apostle Paul urges his readers to "live a life worthy of the Lord and please him in every way" (Colossians 1:10). He then goes on to list a number of ways they could do that, and the *first* thing he mentions is "bearing fruit in every good work."

Paul uses that familiar word *ergon* for "work" here, which, as you likely have memorized by now, means "employment."[27]

He's saying that one of the ways we please God is simply by doing quality work—by serving others through the ministry of excellence.

Jesus alluded to the same principle in his famous parable of the talents about a master who entrusts his wealth to three servants. "To one he gave five bags of gold, to another two bags, and to another one bag" (Matthew 25:15), and then the master goes on a long journey.

Upon his return, he finds that the first servant has diligently put the master's money to work and turned five bags of gold into ten. The second servant produces the same 100 percent return, excellently multiplying two bags of gold into four. So the master turns to the two men and says, "Well done, good and faithful servant! . . . Come and share your master's happiness!" (Matthew 25:21, 23).

The excellent work of the servants leads to joy in the heart of their master. Likewise, our excellent work leads to joy in the heart of the True Master the parable points to. In the words of John Calvin, "No sacrifice is more pleasing to God, than when every man applies diligently to his own calling."[28]

But there are two points of nuance that are important to draw out of this parable before we move on.

First, *Jesus's definition of excellence is much different from the world's.*

The world tends to define excellence as being the best and rising to the top of one's chosen field. But notice that in Jesus's parable the five- and two-talent servants receive the exact same blessing from the master, *even though,* by the world's standards, the five-talent servant is clearly supreme. At the end of the day, he has ten talents, while the other servant has only four. But both are invited to share equally in the master's happiness.

Based on this parable, I think if Jesus were asked to define excellence or success in a word, it would be *stewardship*—doing our best in accordance with the Lord's commands. While the world defines excellence as *being* the best, God seems to define it as *doing* our best. That's what brings him pleasure!

Second, *God calls us to the pursuit of excellence, but not necessarily to the achievement of it.*

The third servant in the parable makes this clear. Unlike the first two servants, who work diligently to steward the resources the master entrusted to them, the third servant buries his treasure in the ground (see Matthew 25:24–25).

But when the master rebukes him, he doesn't say, "I can't believe you didn't produce a 100 percent return like your friends here!" No, he reprimands the servant for being lazy (see verse 26). In other words, the master doesn't admonish the servant for not *achieving* excellence. He rebukes him for not even *trying*.

In his great grace, God never once commands that you and I *attain* any level of excellence at work. But make no mistake about it: The Master finds great joy in watching you *pursue* excellent stewardship of the talents he has given you—especially if you find joy in your work, which brings me to the third way you can bring God eternal pleasure through your job today.

3. Do Work That Brings You Pleasure

As we saw in chapter 1, God issued the First Commission in the context of blessing (see Genesis 1:28). Work was God's first gift to humankind! Now, when you give a gift to your kids, do you expect them to play with the gift grudgingly? Of course not! You want them to find *joy* in the gift. And when they do, it brings *you* joy. So it is with our heavenly Father.

Solomon said, "There is nothing better for people than to eat and drink, and to find enjoyment in their work," because "this ability to find enjoyment comes from God" (Ecclesiastes 2:24, NET). So long as our work is in line with God's commands and pursued with excellence as a means of loving others well, we can feel free from "the tyranny of utility."[29] We can do our work simply for the joy of it, knowing that as we do, we bring great delight to God.

But there are powerful forces that keep us from taking pleasure in our work. Let me quickly address three of them.

First, *many people don't have the opportunity to do what they love on this side of the Fall.*

I have many friends who fall into this camp. If you're one of them, know that I understand your pain and lament with you. Let me remind you of the hope of Isaiah 65:22: A day is coming when you will "long enjoy the work of [your] hands" in the Eternal Heaven on Earth. In the meantime, "work heartily, as for the Lord," knowing that you will receive a reward for your faithfulness (see Colossians 3:23–24, ESV).

Second, *many people are too preoccupied with the work beneath their work to take pleasure in their work.*

After Adam and Eve sinned, "they realized they were naked; so they sewed fig leaves together and made coverings for themselves" to mask their shame (Genesis 3:7). You and I do the same thing today, not with literal fig leaves but with metaphorical ones to be sure. We work ourselves to the point of burnout, often not because we need to financially but because we need to emotionally and spiritually. Because success at work yields one of the largest fig leaves of our modern era—a way to cover the fact that, underneath it all, we aren't really okay.

But of course, that fig leaf inevitably withers, forcing us to work harder to achieve the next level of success all the while sapping the pleasure out of our work. This is what pastor Tim Keller calls the "work beneath the work,"[30] and the only way to escape it is by trusting that Christ alone can take away our shame and insecurities. And once we rest in him, we're free to enjoy our work and bring pleasure to God as we do. Keller explains:

> Christians . . . have been set free to enjoy working. If we begin to *work as if we were serving* the Lord, we will be freed from both overwork and underwork. Neither the prospect of money and acclaim, nor the lack of it, will be our controlling consideration. Work will be primarily a way to please God.[31]

Finally, *many of us are blocked from experiencing God-glorifying pleasure in our work because we have fallen for the lie that our salvation requires giving up everything that once brought us joy.*

This was precisely the struggle Chassie Anders experienced! But check out what the apostle Paul says in 2 Corinthians 5:17: "If anyone is in Christ, he is a new creation" (ESV). And that means that *every* part of us has been made new—including our passions and interests. As Andrew Scott explains,

> God has put in every one of us strong feelings for certain things. Some . . . are passionate about art, others sports. Some love nature, some adventure, others history, animals, figuring out complex technology, singing, running, writing, the list goes on. When we are doing these things, we feel alive. . . . And so it should be because these were given by God.[32]

The world doesn't need more grumpy Christians trudging through life. The world needs Christians who ooze exuberant joy that gives evidence of the abundant life found in Christ alone. Which is why theologian Howard Thurman once said, "Ask yourself what makes you come alive, and go do that, because what the world needs is people who have come alive."[33]

Now again, many of us don't have the option to do "what makes [us] come alive." And our ability to serve others through the ministry of excellence should always take priority over "following our passions."* But if you *are* serving others with excellence in a job that you love, don't feel guilty for that. *Praise God* for that good gift! Because when you do work that brings you pleasure, you also bring pleasure to God.

Here's the fourth way you can bring eternal pleasure to God as you work today.

4. *Work* with *God and Not Just* for *Him*

George Washington Carver felt called by God "to use his agricultural knowledge to help poor black farmers."[34] And he succeeded *massively* in that effort. "Carver's ideas about crop rotation would lift innumerable thousands of [those farmers] out of poverty."[35] In recognition of his extraordinary innovations, *Time* magazine called him a "Black Leonardo [da Vinci]."[36]

And while Carver certainly brought God pleasure by doing this work *for* him, it's clear that Carver also brought God pleasure by working *with* his Creator. "Every morning, [he] took a walk by himself, talking to God and ever on the lookout for interesting plant specimens,"[37] which he called "little windows through which God permits me to commune with him."[38]

---

* See chapter 1 of my book *Master of One* for much more on this.

Carver appears to have avoided the mistake so many of us make today: the mistake of putting "God's mission ahead of God himself."[39] Of being so preoccupied with the work of the Lord that we neglect our relationship with the Lord.

Like Carver, we would be wise to remember that God has called us not to the First and Great Missions but to the First and Great *Co*-missions—to do our work with the One who commissioned it. Because it's both the *for* and the *with* that bring God pleasure.

Before Christ calls us his co-rulers, he calls us his co-heirs and children (see Revelation 21:7; 22:5). As Makoto Fujimura puts it, "We are not [simply] tools to accomplish God's purposes; we are the Bride of Christ."[40] So we can know that just communing with God as we work brings him pleasure.

Maybe this is why our heavenly Father called us to work with him in the first place. God could have fulfilled the First Commission—the call to fill, subdue, and rule this world—*far* more efficiently and effectively on his own. Yet he invites us to do that work with him. Why? Because fathers take great delight in being with and working with their children.

I was reminded of this the other day when my daughter Ellison asked if she could help me grind some coffee beans. Now, you should know that I put the *A* in *type A*. I *hate* messes and inefficiencies, and I knew that if I allowed my seven-year-old to help me, this project was going to take a lot longer and leave a much bigger mess than if I had ground the coffee beans on my own.* But I invited her to help me anyway. Why? *Because she's my daughter* and simply being with her brings me far more joy than a clean countertop.

The same is true with our heavenly Father. "God does not

---

* If you've seen the episode of *Bluey* called "Omelette," you know what I'm talking about.

need us. He wants us."[41] So just being with him as we work brings him pleasure.

The apostle Paul understood this deeply. Even though he was one of the most missionally minded people in history, Paul knew that while God's commissions are of great importance, they aren't of the *greatest* importance. Our mission is penultimate rather than ultimate.

Paul said, "I consider everything a loss because of the surpassing worth of *knowing* Christ Jesus my Lord" (Philippians 3:8). In his terrific book *With,* Skye Jethani explains that, "When [Paul] wrote of 'knowing' Christ, the word did not mean an intellectual knowledge *about* someone, but rather an intimate and *experiential* knowledge. This personal connection with Christ is what Paul valued above all else."[42]

And so, while "God's mission dominated [Paul's] life, it did not define it."[43] Jethani goes on to say that Paul's "communion *with* Christ rooted and preceded his work *for* him."[44] And that surely brought God great pleasure. As the Lord said in Jeremiah 9:24, "Let him who glories glory in this, that he understands and *knows* me . . . for in these things I delight" (RSV).

Want to bring God pleasure as you work today? Work *with* him and not just *for* him. Talk to him, be mindful of his presence, and ask for his help as you go about your day.

Okay, there's one final way to bring God eternal pleasure for us to explore.

5. *Wonder at God's Work While You Work*

On Christmas Eve 1968, a *billion* people sat in front of their TVs and radios—"more people . . . than had ever tuned in to a human voice at once."[45] The voices they were waiting for were those of the crew of *Apollo 8*—the first human beings to ever orbit the moon.

Until an hour before the broadcast, the astronauts weren't sure what they would say to the earthlings back home. Given the date, they had considered "invoking Santa Claus" or "changing the words to 'Jingle Bells,'" but these messages clearly lacked the gravitas this monumental moment called for.[46]

Finally, with the world sitting on the edge of their seats, the astronauts went live and said this: "In the beginning, God created the heavens and the earth."[47] And for a moment, the world stared in wonder at the glory of God's creation.

The crew of *Apollo 8* could have easily used the broadcast to boast in humankind's extraordinary achievement, but instead, they took time to wonder at God's. And that moment was nothing less than praise that undoubtedly brought the Creator cosmic joy.

You and I can do the same today as we take time to wonder at God's work while we work. When we marvel at the natural materials God has given us to create with, praise him for the "coincidence" that helped us land that new hire, or simply stare at the sunset the Creator painted outside our office window, we can know that all of this brings God pleasure. Because we're taking time to assign credit where credit is due—to "ascribe to the LORD the glory due his name" (Psalm 29:2).

Let me give you an example of what this looks like for those of us who aren't astronauts flying through the heavens. When I was writing chapter 2 of this book, I was reminded of the scene in *Moana* where Maui steals the heart of Te Fiti.[48] I couldn't remember all the details of the scene, so I pulled open Disney+, found the movie, and clicked play. And the movie started playing *at the exact scene* I was looking for.

Of course, this wasn't a coincidence. This was clearly God working while I was working. And by taking thirty seconds to stop, marvel at his power, and thank him for the reminder of his presence, I believe I brought him pleasure.

Now, you may be thinking, *Jordan, that's a wild (albeit ridiculous) story. But how in the world does that fleeting moment matter for eternity? How is it "not in vain"?* Because God will remember.

Hebrews 6:10 says that "[God] will not forget your work and the love you have shown him." He won't forget *a single thing* we do in this life that brings him pleasure. And my guess is that those memories will fuel many of our interactions with Christ in the Eternal Heaven on Earth.

I want you to imagine with me for a moment that you are on the New Earth, working at your perfect, eternal vocation, when, all of a sudden, Jesus pulls up a chair and says, "Hey, Jack, do you remember that time, back in the former age, when you hated your job as a server but you obeyed my command to work with excellence for my sake? I remember that. I'm so proud of you."

Or maybe he'll say, "You know, Olivia, I'll never forget the look on my Father's face when we saw you take the natural talents we gave you as an entrepreneur and develop them. You pursued excellence for my glory instead of yours, and we had a blast watching you do it!"

Maybe Jesus will pop into Chassie Anders's salon in the New Jerusalem and say, "I'll never forget the joy on your face when you styled hair and leaned into the work I made you to do, Chassie. You felt my pleasure because it was *real.*"

Or maybe Jesus will approach Victor Boutros at the feast of the Lamb and say, "Victor, you did so much for this kingdom when you spent the former life prosecuting human traffickers. But do you know what brought me even greater joy? The fact that you did it *with* me."

Maybe Jesus will visit the crew of *Apollo 8* as they're gearing up to explore the New Heavens and say, "You guys had every opportunity to orbit the moon and boast in yourselves. But instead, you boasted in me. Well done, good and faithful servants. Come and share your Master's happiness."

Obeying the Lord's commands, pursuing excellence in our work, doing work that brings us pleasure, working with God and not just for him, taking time to wonder at the Lord's work while we work—all of these things bring pleasure to God. And so they are not in vain, because God remembers them for eternity.

But not only will these acts of faithfulness contribute to God's eternal pleasure; they will also determine our eternal rewards. That's the subject of our next chapter.

YOUR SACRED RESPONSE

As we saw in this chapter, one of the ways we bring God eternal pleasure is by doing our work *with* him and not just *for* him. But I know it can be really tough to know what that looks like practically. We work with mostly visible things and yet worship "the invisible God" (Colossians 1:15).

How can we be mindful of his presence throughout the day? Here's one idea: Create an email address for your prayers.

Let me explain.

When my friend Jenna Barrett was doing an internship at Hilton, she wanted a practical way to bring God into her work in a big corporate office. On my podcast, she said, "I can't necessarily just pull out my Bible, but I created an email [address] so I could email God my prayers, and so during meetings, if I'd just gotten a project and I didn't know how to handle it, I would email him just like he was my co-worker and ask for advice and pray and ask for wisdom."[49]

I *love* the simplicity and genius of this practice. You probably spend a lot of time sending emails, texts, and other messages at work. By creating a way to send messages "to God," you'll be making his presence much more tangible and real, thus increasing the chances you'll do your work with him and bring him eternal pleasure.

If this practice sounds brilliant to you, take five minutes right now to create your own private email address for your prayers via a free service like Gmail. If this practice sounds crazy to you, download *The Sacred Response* workbook at jordanraynor.com/response to find alternative practices for bringing God pleasure while you work like identifying opportunities for greater obedience and creating visible reminders of God's invisible presence.

4

HOW TO MAXIMIZE YOUR ETERNAL REWARDS AND ENSURE YOUR WORK *PHYSICALLY* LASTS INTO HEAVEN

J.R.R. Tolkien was despondent after a neighbor unexpectedly cut back one of his favorite trees. And while Tolkien certainly missed the tree's former glory, it wasn't the tree itself that was the real cause of his misery. It was what Tolkien feared the mutilated tree represented: namely, that his "internal Tree"—his magnum opus, *The Lord of the Rings*—would soon meet the same fate.[1]

World War II was just beginning, and while there was no chance the forty-six-year-old Tolkien would be drafted into service, his memories of fighting in the First World War were enough to remind him of the fragility of life—even for private citizens.

By this time, Tolkien had already spent *years* working on the massively intricate mythology that was the background for the *Lord of the Rings* saga. Now he was plagued by the "dreadful and numbing thought" that, like his beloved tree, his life's work might be cut short and "in the end he would achieve nothing."[2]

As an act of defiance, therapy, or some combination of the two, Tolkien decided to write his way out of his personal crisis by penning a short autobiographical parable called "Leaf by Niggle." Niggle was an artist who was working on a painting of a leaf. But much like Tolkien's own vision for his creative work, Niggle's vision for his painting expanded greatly. What once was just a single leaf grew into a vision for an enormous tree with giant roots and countless branches—and beyond the tree a beautiful landscape with snowcapped mountains.[3]

Niggle worked diligently on his grand painting, but he had a difficult time making progress on account of his perfectionism and his sense of duty to his neighbors, who were often in need of his help.[4]

One day, when Niggle *finally* found some time to work, a man appeared at his door with some grave news. "You start today on your journey," the man said.[5] Niggle knew precisely what the man meant. The journey this man was referring to was Niggle's own death.

But Niggle was far from ready to leave behind his life and his life's work. Standing there in front of his incomplete masterpiece, Niggle wept over the apparent vanity of his labor. "Oh, dear!" he cried. "And it's not even finished!"[6]

After Niggle died, his painting was almost completely destroyed by weather. But one of his neighbors stumbled upon a fragment and was able to preserve "one beautiful leaf" from the canvas.[7] The neighbor had the small painting framed and placed in a museum. But eventually the museum burnt down, and Niggle and his work were entirely forgotten.[8]

Depressing story, huh? If Tolkien weren't a devout Christian, the story may have ended there. But thankfully, it doesn't.

Tolkien tells us that after death knocked on Niggle's door, the painter was sent on a train to a heavenly afterlife. There we see Niggle bicycling through an idyllic countryside resembling the Eternal Heaven on Earth when, all of a sudden, something caught his eye that was so startling that he fell off his bike.

"Before him stood the Tree, his Tree, finished . . . its leaves opening, its branches growing and bending in the wind that Niggle had so often felt or guessed, and had so often failed to catch."[9] Niggle's labor wasn't in vain after all. His vision was standing right before his eyes more perfect and real than he could have ever imagined. Staring at the tree, Niggle lifted his arms to the heavens and exclaimed, "It's a gift!"[10]

Over the years, Tolkien fans have offered many interpretations of this beautiful parable. But I think Tolkien's biographer Tom Shippey got it right when he said that this tree is "Niggle's reward" for a life well lived and work well done.[11] I think Tolkien was trying to convey a truth we see throughout Scripture—namely, that one of the ways our work matters for eternity is that God will judge and reward it—even by miraculously carrying some of the literal work of our hands into the Eternal Heaven on Earth.

WHAT GOD MAY ASK YOU WHEN HE JUDGES YOUR WORK

When we think of God's judgment, most of us think primarily or even exclusively of God judging our souls. And it's true, of course, that each person's soul will be judged. But, praise God, "there is now no condemnation for those who are in Christ Jesus" (Romans 8:1). If you are in Christ, your soul *has* been judged—past tense—and there is *nothing* you can do to lose your salvation (see Romans 8:38–39).

But Scripture makes it clear that it's not just our souls that God will examine. Every person—including Christians—will be judged "for everything we do" in this life (Ecclesiastes 12:14, NLT). Which is why "we must *all* appear before the judgment seat of Christ" in the end (2 Corinthians 5:10, ESV).

And since we spend such an enormous chunk of our lives working, we can assume that much of Christ's judgment will focus on our vocations. Peter speaks to this explicitly, saying that God will judge "each person's work impartially" (1 Peter 1:17).

When you meet your Maker, he will likely ask you questions about how you worked in this life. Using our biblically informed imaginations, we can guess that those questions might include the following:*

- "Did you 'give thanks in all circumstances' at work, even the difficult ones I allowed?" (see 1 Thessalonians 5:18).
- "Did you do your work with excellence, even when your bosses weren't watching?" (see Ephesians 6:5–6).
- "Did you show mercy to your team members the way that I showed you mercy?" (see Luke 6:36).

What will the purpose of questions like these be? Why will God judge the work of his children? Not to decide where we will spend eternity, but to determine which rewards we will enjoy for eternity: "We must all appear before the judgment seat of Christ, *so that* each one may receive what is due for what he has done" (2 Corinthians 5:10, ESV). Here Paul is echoing Jesus, who promised that "the Son of Man is going to come in his Father's glory with his angels, and then he will reward each person according to what they have done" (Matthew 16:27).

That truth points us to perhaps the most tangible of the four ways your work matters for eternity:

Way 2: Your work matters for eternity because it is largely through your work that you earn eternal rewards.

Before we go any further, I want you to stop and marvel with me at the *absurdity* of God's goodness. We were once God's enemies, deserving of death because of our sin (see Ro-

---

* You can see more questions like these to help you prejudge your work today in *The Sacred Response* workbook, which you can download for free at jordan raynor.com/response.

mans 6:23). But God chose to show us unfathomable mercy and carry out the punishment for *our* sins on *his* sinless Son so that we could be saved!

And as we saw in chapter 1, while Christ hasn't redeemed us *by* our good works, he has saved us *for* them. One of the purposes of our salvation is "to do good works, which God prepared in advance for us to do"—namely, the First and Great Commissions (see Ephesians 2:8–10).

The fact that God saved us from eternal separation from him should be more than enough to motivate us to do these good works. But God knew that *even after he saved us from eternal death,* we would still be deeply selfish—tempted to focus on our own kingdoms rather than his. So, in his unmatched goodness and generosity, God offers us eternal rewards to motivate us to do his will.

Now, I know some of you have your hand raised right now and are wanting to say, "Jordan, it just feels *wrong* to be motivated by eternal rewards." I see that hand. I hear you. And I used to understand that feeling all too well. So before we explore *what* rewards Scripture promises (which, trust me, are going to blow your mind) and *how* we can obtain them, let me make a case for *why* we should boldly chase after eternal rewards in the first place.

THREE REASONS TO UNASHAMEDLY CHASE AFTER ETERNAL REWARDS

1. Jesus Told You To

Over and over and over again (see Matthew 5:11–12, 19; 6:1–4, 6, 17–20, 33; 10:41–42; 16:27; 19:27–30; 25:14–30, 34–40; Mark 9:41; Luke 6:22–23, 35, 38; 12:33; 14:12–14; Revelation 2:10, 17, 23, 26–28; 22:12).

If Jesus didn't want us to be motivated by eternal rewards, then why in the world did he spend *so* much time talking about them? C. S. Lewis was right when he said that "if we consider the unblushing promises of reward and the staggering nature of the rewards promised in the Gospels, it would seem that Our Lord finds our desires not too strong, but too weak."[12]

Well, Jordan, Jesus motivates us with rewards, but ultimately we're going to lay all of them back down at his feet, right? Some of them, sure (see Revelation 4:10–11)! But pay close attention to Jesus's words in Matthew 6:20. He said, "Store up *for yourselves* treasures in heaven"—not "Store up *for God* treasures in heaven."

Commenting on this verse, Randy Alcorn says that while it "may sound selfish" to chase after eternal rewards, "it is Christ's command to us, so we should eagerly obey it. . . . If we maintain that it's wrong to be motivated by rewards, we bring a serious accusation against Christ!"[13]

Still not convinced? Here's the second reason we should be motivated to pursue eternal rewards.

2. Rewards Are Repayment

It's natural to feel guilty about being motivated by rewards if we fail to recognize that Scripture almost always ties the promise of rewards to things God calls us to sacrifice in the present. Listen to Jesus's exchange with his disciples in Matthew 19:

> Peter [said], "We have left everything to follow you! What then will there be for us?"
>
> Jesus said to them, "Truly I tell you, at the renewal of all things, when the Son of Man sits on his glorious

throne, you who have followed me will also sit on twelve thrones, judging the twelve tribes of Israel. And everyone who has left houses or brothers or sisters or father or mother or wife or children or fields for my sake will receive a hundred times as much and will inherit eternal life. (Matthew 19:27–29)

Jesus didn't say, "How *dare* you ask me about rewards, Peter? I've come to save your life! Isn't that enough?" No, Jesus implied that the disciples were *right* to ask about their eternal rewards and that the granting of said rewards will be an act of *justice*.

The same is true for you and me. Hebrews 6:10 says that "God is *not unjust;* he will not forget your work and the love you have shown him." In Revelation 22:12, Jesus said, "I am coming soon, bringing my *recompense* with me, to *repay* each one for what he has done" (ESV). Jeremiah 17:10 quotes God as saying, "I the LORD . . . reward each person according to their conduct, according to what their deeds *deserve.*"

Now, I have to stop here and say how much I *hate* the word *deserve* as it's typically used. When my daughter Kate turned six, she said, "Daddy, Gigi owes me a trip to Build-A-Bear!" Sensing an opportunity to teach my child a lesson about grace, I said, "Kate, nobody *owes* you a thing. The only thing you and I deserve is death because of our sin. Everything else is—" "But, Dad," Kate interrupted, "look at this card from Gigi. It says, 'I *owe* you a trip to Build-A-Bear!'"

Face, meet palm. I felt like an idiot. But my point still stands. You and I don't deserve a single thing in *this* life. But if we give up this life for the sake of Christ and his gospel, Scripture says we *do* deserve rewards in the *next* life. This is what proponents of the perverted and heretical prosperity gospel get wrong. Jesus didn't promise us our best life *now*.[14] But he *did* promise us our best life *later*. Why? Because "true Christianity is a fight."[15]

As John Eldredge puts it, "God seems to be of the opinion that no one should be expected to sustain the rigors of the Christian life without very *robust* and *concrete* hopes of being brazenly rewarded for it."[16]

That's the second reason we should unashamedly chase after eternal rewards. Here's the third.

3. The Greater Your Rewards, the Greater God's Glory

The whole point of eternity is for God to receive the glory due his name. Our rewards will serve that purpose in at least two ways.

First, *we will lay some of our rewards down at the feet of Jesus as acts of worship* (see Isaiah 60:1–7).

Second, *any rewards we hold on to will bring Christ greater glory because they will serve as tangible reminders that Jesus was worth far more than whatever we sacrificed in this life.*

I'll unpack this idea more at the end of this chapter, but first we must explore what exactly these eternal rewards are that God has offered us. You're probably familiar with Scripture's promise of "treasures in heaven" (Matthew 6:20) and various crowns (see 1 Corinthians 9:25–27; 1 Thessalonians 2:19; 2 Timothy 4:8; James 1:12; 1 Peter 5:4; Revelation 2:10). So let's take a closer look at four less explored rewards to fuel our faithfulness and hope in the present.

FOUR ETERNAL REWARDS BEYOND TREASURES AND CROWNS

1. Words of Affirmation

Aarti Sequeira has a lot on her plate as a wife, mother, author, chef, and Food Network star. But the work beneath all that work is singular. "When I reach the end of my days," Sequeira says, "all I want is to hear the Lord say, 'Well done good and faithful servant.'"[17]

Sequeira understands a truth we saw in the previous chapter—namely, that "the smile of God is the goal of your life."[18] But she also knows that some of us will see a bigger, broader smile based on how we steward this life.

That smile—and the words God speaks over you once his smile appears—will be among your greatest eternal rewards. That's clearly one of the points of the parable of the talents, where the master's famous words of affirmation are given as a reward for his servants' faithfulness (see Matthew 25:14–30).

After God judges *your* work, what will he say to *you*? Will he have nothing to affirm in your life other than trusting in his Son? Or will he shout loud enough for all to hear, "This is my child, in whom I am well pleased! Well done, good and faithful servant!"

Our work today will directly influence the words of affirmation we hear for eternity. It will also dictate what you and I wear.

2. Threads in Our Wedding Dress

Scripture frequently refers to Christians who make up the global church as the bride of Christ.[19] And in Revelation

19:7–8, John provides us with a surprising detail as to how that bride's wedding dress will be made: "'The wedding of the Lamb has come, and his bride has made herself ready. Fine linen, bright and clean, was given her to wear.' (Fine linen stands for the righteous acts of God's holy people.)"

Hold up a minute. Wait. Our good works—our "righteous acts"—somehow become part of the *clothing* we'll wear when we meet Jesus? That seems to be what John is saying. Randy Alcorn explains,

> Each prayer, each gift, each hour of fasting, each kindness to the needy, all of these are the threads that have been woven together into this wedding dress. Her works have been empowered by the Spirit, and she has spent her life on Earth sewing her wedding dress for the day when she will be joined to her beloved Bridegroom.[20]

Are these threads in our wedding dress literal or metaphorical? Nobody knows. I love to think they're literal, kind of like in *Frozen II* when all those ice crystals gel together to form Elsa's dress.

But metaphorical or literal, the point remains the same: Our work matters for eternity because every good work we do will be rewarded with another thread in our wedding gown. Which should be incredibly motivating for those of us who don't want to show up to the wedding of the Lamb scantily clad.

While our entrance into the proverbial chapel is secure regardless of our good works, how we show up there isn't. Neither is the work we get to do, which brings me to the third eternal reward I want us to explore.

3. Increased Job Responsibilities

As we saw in chapter 2, Joni Eareckson Tada longs to paint "big splashy murals" in the Eternal Heaven on Earth.[21] But Tada recognizes that the job she has in the *next* life is contingent on how she works in *this* one. "Everything we do down here on earth," Tada says, "either increases our capacity for joy and worship and work and service in heaven or it decreases that capacity."[22]

What's Tada talking about? She's referring to the biblical truth that while every citizen of heaven will equally "enjoy the work of their hands" (Isaiah 65:22), not all of that work will be created equal. Because as Jesus made clear, one of our eternal rewards is increased job responsibilities for eternity (see Matthew 19:28–30).

This is one of the lessons of Jesus's parable of the minas (see Luke 19:11–27), which is similar to but certainly distinct from the parable of the talents.[23] Both parables feature a master who represents Jesus. In both parables, the master asks a few servants to steward his money while he goes on a journey.

As we've already seen, the reward for good stewardship in the parable of the talents is words of affirmation. But the reward in the parable of the minas is increased vocational responsibility: " 'Well done, my good servant!' his master replied. 'Because you have been trustworthy in a very small matter, take charge of ten cities'" (Luke 19:17).

The point of the parable is clear: While all Christians share equal *status* as adopted children of God, we will *not* all share equal *station* and responsibility in the Eternal Heaven on Earth. Some will lead, while others follow. Some will rule over great cities, while others sweep the streets. Some may pilot space shuttles to explore the New Heavens, while others remain on the ground.

Joni Eareckson Tada is properly motivated by this incredible reward. "I don't want to be among the least," she says. "I don't want to be in the lesser ranks. I want to do everything I can to be as happy in heaven and as useful to the King as I possibly can."[24]

In a minute, we're going to see exactly how to do everything we can to maximize our heavenly job responsibilities and other eternal rewards. But first there's one more reward I want you to see.

4. *Your Work* Physically *Lasting for Eternity*

This is probably the reward that is talked about least in our churches today. But it's also one of the most inspiring. Because as the playwright Arthur Miller says, "Greater than hunger or sex or thirst" is the innate human desire "to leave a thumbprint somewhere on the world."[25] It's why Tolkien's "Leaf by Niggle" resonates so deeply. We all want our work to *literally* and *physically* last forever.

And that longing is ancient. It's what Moses prayed when he famously asked God to "establish the work of our hands" (Psalm 90:17). The Hebrew word for "establish" there literally means to "make permanent."[26]

Moses, Niggle, *all* of us want God to make permanent the work of our hands. We want our inventions, art, and ideas to last. For our labor to *literally* not be in vain. For it to *physically* survive for eternity.

As we saw in chapter 2, that longing isn't sinful or misguided wishful thinking. It's rooted in something profoundly biblical and true, as seen in the parallel prophetic visions of Isaiah 60:4–9 and Revelation 21:24–26, where God welcomes "the glory and honor of the nations" (ships, incense, and other human culture) into the New Jerusalem (verse 26).

The implication of these prophetic visions is stunning. The novels we write, the inventions we make, the structures we build—all of it has a shot at lasting into the Eternal Heaven on Earth. The world's leading New Testament expert says that "strange though it may seem, almost as hard to believe as the resurrection itself," the work of our hands has a chance of literally lasting *"into God's future."*[27]

This is an *incredibly* motivating reward for construction workers, chefs, and creators like Niggle who make physical things today. But what about those of us who don't? How might the work of a financial adviser, coach, or executive assistant be considered "the glory and honor of the nations" when there are no physical artifacts of your work?

Will there be videos in the elevators of the New Jerusalem showing you refusing to take advantage of a client? Will Jesus share stories of your obedience around one of the New Earth's epic campfires? Will the emails you send in love and without angry haste be cataloged in one of the New Jerusalem's epic libraries? I don't know. But you can take it to the bank that this reward of your work *literally* lasting for eternity is there for you as an incentive.

The question, of course, is this: What work will be considered "the glory and honor of the nations," and what won't? Or asked more generally of *all* the rewards we've explored in this chapter, what exactly can we do to access them?

Here are just seven of the *many* things God says he will reward as we carry out the First and Great Commissions.

HOW TO MAXIMIZE YOUR ETERNAL REWARDS

1. *Work with Gold, Silver, and Costly Stones*

In 1 Corinthians 3:11–15, the apostle Paul says this:

> No one can lay any foundation other than the one al-
> ready laid, which is Jesus Christ. If anyone builds on
> this foundation using gold, silver, costly stones, wood,
> hay or straw, their work will be shown for what it is,
> because the Day will bring it to light. It will be revealed
> with fire, and the fire will test the quality of each per-
> son's work. If what has been built survives, the builder
> will receive a reward. If it is burned up, the builder will
> suffer loss but yet will be saved—even though only as
> one escaping through the flames.

The reward Paul is referring to here could mean any of the
rewards we've explored in this chapter. But given the physical
language Paul is using—especially "if what has been built
survives"—he could be referring specifically to the reward of
our work being deemed the glory of the nations.*

What work does Paul say meets that criteria? Work done
with "gold, silver, [and] costly stones" (verse 12). Paul, of
course, isn't talking about *literal* gold, silver, and stones. So the
question becomes, What do these metaphorical substances
represent?

---

* That's what the theologians behind the *Theology of Work Bible Commentary*
argue. About this passage, one of them says, "This may be the most direct statement of the eternal value of earthly work in all of Scripture. The work we do
on earth—to the extent we do it according to the ways of Christ—survives into
eternity." Joel R. White, "Do Good Work (1 Corinthians 3:10–17)," Theology
of Work Project, December 16, 2011, www.theologyofwork.org/new-
testament/1-corinthians/do-good-work-1-cor-310-17.

I've read dozens of theologians' answers to that question. The *Theology of Work Bible Commentary* says that it will be work done "according to the ways of Christ" and "in excellence, by his gifts and grace," that lasts forever.[28] Theologian Lesslie Newbigin says, "Every faithful act of service, every honest labor to make the world a better place," will survive God's judgment.[29] Skye Jethani believes that it will be "works of high quality" and consistent "with the character of God."[30]

Here's how I'd summarize my own biblically informed guess as to what work will be rewarded with the status of "the glory and honor of the nations": any work we do with excellence, with love, and in accordance with God's commands.

And isn't that precisely what we saw in Tolkien's parable? Niggle didn't just pursue excellence in his craft of painting. He pursued excellence with *love*. He sacrificed his time to show mercy and care to his neighbors "in need of help."[31] Niggle worked with excellence, with love, and in accordance with God's commands. And that, I believe, is why Tolkien shows him being rewarded with the gift of his painting adorning eternity.[32]

Here's the second way we can unlock the eternal rewards we've explored in this chapter.

2. Work Hard

Colossians 3:23–24 says, "Whatever you do, work at it with all your heart, as working for the Lord, not for human masters, since you know that you will receive an inheritance from the Lord as a reward." This one is pretty straightforward. You earn eternal rewards every day you work hard at the work God has given you to do—*especially* when you don't love your job (see Colossians 3:22).

3. Endure Insults Because of Your Allegiance to Christ

In Luke 6:22–23, Jesus said, "Blessed are you when people hate you, when they exclude you and insult you and reject your name as evil, because of the Son of Man. Rejoice in that day and leap for joy, because great is your reward in heaven."

Does a co-worker hate you for your biblically based stance on a certain issue? Has being open about your faith caused industry insiders to exclude you from the cool kids' table? "Rejoice," Jesus said! Because eternal treasures, job promotions, and the other rewards we've explored are coming your way soon.

4. Give to the Poor

Luke 12:33–34 quotes Jesus as saying, "Sell your possessions and give to the poor. Provide purses for yourselves that will not wear out, a treasure in heaven that will never fail, where no thief comes near and no moth destroys. For where your treasure is, there your heart will be also."

In short, give now and be rewarded with much more forever. Which is really not giving as much as it is investing. Proverbs 19:17 gets at this truth: "Whoever is kind to the poor *lends* to the LORD," because "he will reward them for what they have done." The missionary Jim Elliot was right: "He is no fool who gives what he cannot keep to gain that which he cannot lose."[33]

5. Pray

Matthew 6:6 records Jesus as saying this: "When you pray, go into your room, close the door and pray to your Father, who is unseen. Then your Father, who sees what is done in secret, will reward you."

As we saw in chapter 3, we bring God eternal pleasure when we do our work *with* him and not just *for* him. He wants to be with us so much that he rewards us for talking with him throughout the day! But prayer is far from the only way to maximize your eternal rewards. Here's another.

6. *Do Good to Your Enemies*

In Luke 6:35, Jesus said, "Love your enemies, do good to them, and lend to them without expecting to get anything back. Then your reward will be great." This may be the hardest command to obey in this entire list. Jesus isn't calling us to simply avoid harming our enemies. He's calling us to *proactively* "do good" to them!

What does this look like in practice? It could look like picking up coffee for the vendor who's suing you before your next deposition. Or praying for the prosperity of your conniving co-worker. Or contacting the company who's knocking off your product and offering to help them create a unique one.

Those actions make *zero* sense to the world. But they make all the sense in the world for those following Jesus and chasing after the eternal rewards he has promised.

7. *Offer Hospitality to Those Who Can't Repay You*

Luke 14:12–14 records Jesus as saying, "When you give a luncheon or dinner, do not invite your friends, your brothers or sisters, your relatives, or your rich neighbors; if you do, they may invite you back and so you will be repaid. But when you give a banquet, invite the poor, the crippled, the lame, the blind, and you will be blessed. Although they cannot repay you, you will be repaid at the resurrection of the righteous."

Many of us have opportunities to practice this at work daily. Instead of having lunch with your boss who can promote you, have lunch with an intern who "cannot repay you" or serve you in any way. Instead of giving preferential service to the table most likely to give you the biggest tip, give exceptional service to everyone who dines in your restaurant. And know that when you do, you'll be storing up for yourself the rewards we've been exploring in this chapter.

This list of seven ways to earn eternal rewards is far from exhaustive. Which is why I love how broadly Paul sums things up, saying, "The Lord will reward each one for *whatever* good they do" (Ephesians 6:8). *Whatever* you do for God's glory and the good of others—big or small—matters for eternity.

Does that mean I'll be rewarded for leaving the last Topo Chico in the refrigerator for my wife this morning? Maybe! Well, probably not, since I've no longer done that in secret (see Matthew 6:1–4), but you get my point: Every single action you take today has an impact on the treasure, crowns, words of affirmation, clothing, and vocation you'll be rewarded with in the Eternal Heaven on Earth. And every one of those rewards will serve as a reminder that Jesus was more than worth whatever you sacrificed in the present age.

Have you sacrificed profits in order to pay your employees a wage that allows them and their families to flourish? A day is coming when you'll stare at your heavenly treasure and remember that Jesus was worth it!

Have you laid down your dream job so your spouse can have theirs? A day is coming when you'll be a million years into *your* dream job and remember that Jesus was worth it!

Are you, like Niggle, sacrificing progress on your magnum

opus so that you can care for the needs in your community? A day is coming when you'll ride the ships of Tarshish with your finished masterpiece in hand and remember that Jesus was worth it!

One final word before we turn to chapter 5 to see the next way your work matters for eternity. In all of this talk about rewards, it can be easy to lose sight of the fact that while eternal rewards will vary widely from Christian to Christian, our eternal status as co-heirs with Christ will not.

Read Paul's words in 1 Corinthians 3 one more time. He says that if our work is "burned up" by God's fire of judgment (that is, if our work is found undeserving of rewards), "the builder will suffer loss *but yet will be saved*—even though only as one escaping through the flames" (1 Corinthians 3:15).

Romans 10:9 promises, "If you confess with your mouth that Jesus is Lord and believe in your heart that God raised him from the dead, you *will be saved*" (esv). Period. Full stop.

But may the security of that salvation never lead us to coast toward eternity. May we not enter heaven "only as one escaping through the flames." May our salvation lead us to be *wildly* ambitious for doing as many good works as possible to acquire as many rewards as possible for God's glory and our eternal joy!

YOUR SACRED RESPONSE

The concept of a bucket list has always rubbed me the wrong way. Not because I don't love cheesy Morgan Freeman movies, but because the whole idea assumes that the only chance we have to enjoy the best places, food, and experiences this world has to offer is before we die and "kick the bucket." But everything we saw in chapter 2 totally debunks that thinking!

To be clear, there's nothing necessarily wrong with creating a bucket list. But given what we saw in this chapter and chapter 2, I think more Christians need to create *anti*-bucket lists: catalogs of things we'll strive *not* to do on this side of eternity so that we can accumulate as many eternal rewards as possible. Because almost every reward Scripture promises is tied to sacrifices we make in the present.

Let me give you a personal example to illustrate this concept. Beyond God's Word, prayer, and musical worship, nothing fuels my soul more than great cities. Every time I visit London, Washington, D.C., or some other world-class city, I want to move there. Not because I don't *love* my hometown of Tampa, Florida. I do. But my soul *craves* being able to walk to work, restaurants, church, the park, etc.

So why don't I move my family to one of these world-class cities? There are many reasons, but one of the top ones is that my aging parents as well as my wife's parents are within a ten-minute drive of our current home and we want to be here to help care for them as they get older.

That's a massive sacrifice for me personally (less so for my *far* less selfish wife). If I were living for this life alone, "Move our family to Washington, D.C." would be near the top of my bucket list.

But knowing that heaven will ultimately be on earth and that we'll have all of eternity to explore the greatest city of all time, I put this item on my anti-bucket list, because I'm confident that the Lord will reward me "for whatever good [I] do" for his glory and the good of others (Ephesians 6:8).

Will my eternal rewards include the urban flat I've always dreamed of in the New Jerusalem? Who knows? But I *do* know that God will reward my faithfulness in ways that make my current sacrifice seem infinitesimally small in retrospect.

In response to this chapter, I want to encourage you to start your own anti-bucket list. If you're looking for inspiration, I've shared several more examples from my own list in *The Sacred Response* workbook, which you can download for free at jordanraynor.com/response. There you'll also find plenty of space to create your own anti-bucket list as well as two other practices to help you maximize the eternal rewards you're earning through your work: judging your work before God does and optimizing a specific project to be deemed "the glory and honor of the nations."

5

HOW TO SCRATCH OFF THE KINGDOM OF GOD AND YANK PIECES OF HEAVEN ONTO EARTH

C. S. Lewis was a fully committed atheist by the age of sixteen. As one of his biographers explains, "The rational case for religion was, in Lewis's view, totally bankrupt."[1]

But something other than reason persistently nagged at Lewis, causing some part of him to long for more than what logic could provide. "He continued to find himself experiencing deep feelings of desire" through "momentary and transient epiphanies," which left "nothing but a memory and a longing."[2]

The most significant of these moments took place while Lewis was waiting for a train on a frosty afternoon in England.[3] To combat his boredom, the young man browsed through the train station's bookstore until a novel called *Phantastes* caught his eye.[4] As he slid his money across the checkout counter, he had no idea that this novel was about to change his life forever.

Reading *Phantastes* was, for Lewis, "not only a literary experience but a spiritual one as well," another biographer explains.[5] There was something so beautiful, true, and transcendent about this novel that it caused a hairline fracture in Lewis's atheism. "He had discovered a 'new quality,' a 'bright shadow,' which seemed to him like a voice calling him from the ends of the earth."[6]

Reflecting on this experience years later, Lewis wrote, "I did not yet know (and I was long in learning) the name of the new quality. . . . I do now. It was Holiness."[7] That day as Lewis began to read, he caught a glimpse of the eternal kingdom of God.

What Lewis couldn't know at the time was that this glimpse was no accident. It had been intentionally planted in *Phantastes* by the book's author, George MacDonald, a pastor turned novelist. As one writer explains in a biographical sketch, MacDonald "never saw [his novels] primarily as entertainment but as a way of communicating his vision of the immensity of God's love."[8]

But not explicitly. MacDonald seems to have understood that if he tacked on a Romans Road tract to the end of his novels, teenagers like Lewis wouldn't pick them up in the first place. His goal in his writings was not to instantly convert, but "to evoke a sense of wonder in the reader, reminding us that there is more to the world than meets the eye. MacDonald shows us a world where the boundary between the seen and the unseen is very thin indeed."[9]

THE THIN VEIL SEPARATING HEAVEN AND EARTH

As we saw in chapter 2, the kingdom of heaven (aka the kingdom of God) isn't just a place we go in the future. It's a place *and* a state of affairs that is breaking into the present.

It may be helpful to think of heaven as a hidden dimension of our world. As leading New Testament scholar N. T. Wright explains, heaven is not "a place miles up in the sky" but "God's dimension of reality which intersects with ours."[10] Heaven and earth "are not two different locations within the same continuum of space or matter. They are two different dimensions of God's good creation."[11] Kind of like Narnia and England or Platform 9 ¾ and King's Cross Station.

And while "the present Heaven is normally invisible to those living on Earth,"[12] it's not always invisible. Jesus "saw heaven being torn open" at his baptism (Mark 1:10). Stephen saw "heaven open" before he was martyred (Acts 7:56). Elisha's servant "saw the hills full of horses and chariots of fire" when God lifted the veil, allowing him a glimpse into the dimension of heaven (2 Kings 6:17).

Biblical accounts like these make clear that heaven isn't as far off as we often think. It's right beside us, hiding behind "an invisible screen, but present and real."[13] And while God alone can literally and physically lift the veil between heaven and earth, C. S. Lewis's encounter with *Phantastes* shows us that human work can figuratively and mysteriously do the same thing.

Our work can create what Celtic Christians call "'thin places' . . . where the curtain between heaven and earth seems almost transparent"[14]—experiences that "trigger a sense of being swept into a timeless moment, a place where time stands still and the breath of eternity rustles through our hearts and minds."[15]

Indeed, this is what much of Jesus's own work accomplished. When he fed the five thousand, he created a thin place of sorts, offering a preview of the day when God's people "will neither hunger nor thirst" (Isaiah 49:10). When he miraculously helped Peter haul in a record catch of fish, he allowed us to steal a glimpse of the day when we will all "long enjoy the work of [our] hands" and "not labor in vain" (Isaiah 65:22–23). And when he rose from the dead, he pulled the firstfruits of resurrection through the veil, giving us a foretaste of what's promised for everyone who is in Christ (see 1 Corinthians 15:20–23).

Commenting on scenes like these, Dr. Amy Sherman says that "it is as though [Jesus] was reaching into the new heavens and new earth . . . and yanking a foretaste of that back into the present."[16]

But that work of yanking pieces of heaven onto earth didn't stop with Jesus. As we saw in chapter 1, God chose to continue the work of slowly unveiling his kingdom through you and me.

Now, there's lots of language thrown around the church today about the role we humans play in the kingdom of God. Some say that we build or grow the kingdom,[17] but those verbs aren't quite accurate, because the kingdom is God's creation alone. "The kingdom is what it is," say pastors Kevin DeYoung and Greg Gilbert. "It does not expand. It does not increase. It does not grow."[18]

So, if you and I don't grow the kingdom, what role *do* we play? Pastor Tim Keller says that we "*spread* the kingdom."[19] Another leading theologian says we're called to "*model and display*" the kingdom.[20] DeYoung and Gilbert say that we cause the kingdom to "*break in* more and more," kind of like the sun peeking through clouds.[21]

These are all different ways of saying the same thing: While God alone *builds* his kingdom, your life and work can *reveal* more and more of it in the present.

Let me offer an analogy to make this fairly amorphous concept more concrete: a scratch-off. Now, before you flood me with angry emails, rest assured that I'm not talking about the scratch-offs used to play the lottery. I'm referring to the scratch-off paper our kids love that leaves black residue all over our homes.

On the surface, these scratch-offs look like dull pieces of black paper. But when our kids rub the surface with a stylus or a coin, the thin dark veil fades away, revealing a beautiful picture on the other side.

That's a pretty good image of what George MacDonald's novel did for C. S. Lewis and what our work can do today. Through our jobs, we can serve as a stylus of sorts, scratching off the darkness of this world and revealing glimpses of the eternal kingdom of God.

In part 2 of this book, I'm showing you four ways your work matters for eternity. This picture of a scratch-off brings us to the third:

Way 3: Your work matters for eternity because through it you can scratch off the veil between heaven and earth, revealing glimpses of the kingdom of God in the present.

The question, then, is, What is hiding on the underside of the scratch-off? Said another way, What are the attributes of the eternal kingdom of God that you and I are called to unveil? When God removes the veil between heaven and earth once and for all, here's what Scripture says we can expect to see on the other side:

- perfect relationship with God (see Revelation 21:3)
- perfect relationships with other people (see Psalm 46:9; Micah 4:3; Revelation 7:9–17)
- justice (see Isaiah 30:18; 61:8)
- beauty (see Isaiah 35; Revelation 21:9–21)
- order (see 1 Corinthians 14:33)
- abundance (see Isaiah 25:6–9; 49:10; 65:22; Joel 3:18)
- humility (see Matthew 19:30)

- cultural excellence (see Isaiah 60; Revelation 21:26)
- physical health (see Isaiah 32:3–4; 35:6; Revelation 21:4)
- joy (see Isaiah 65:17–18; Revelation 21:4)
- safety (see Isaiah 65:21; Ezekiel 34:28; Micah 4:4)
- sense of belonging (see Psalm 68:6)
- freedom from anxiety (see Isaiah 32:4)
- work we love to do (see Isaiah 65:22–23)
- sustainable earth (see Isaiah 51:3; Revelation 11:15–18)[22]

I'd be foolish to call this a comprehensive list given that "no eye has seen, no ear has heard, and no mind has imagined what God has prepared for those who love him" (1 Corinthians 2:9, NLT). But this gives us a pretty good idea of what the kingdom of God is like. If I were forced to sum it up in a single word, it would be the Hebrew word *shalom*—"the way things ought to be" and one day *will* be when the veil between heaven and earth is completely removed.[23]

Until then, we're called to scratch off glimpses of shalom—glimpses of the kingdom—on this side of the veil. Pastor John Mark Comer puts it this way:

> We're called to a very specific kind of work. To make a Garden-like world where image bearers can flourish and thrive, where people can experience and enjoy God's generous love. A kingdom where God's will is done "on earth as it is in heaven," *where the glass wall between earth and heaven is so thin and clear and translucent that you don't even remember it's there.*[24]

Amen. But *how*? Here are three ways.

HOW TO SCRATCH OFF THE KINGDOM OF GOD

1. *Weed Out What Doesn't Belong in the Kingdom*

The rightful king of France had yet to be crowned. This was a grave injustice in the eyes of Joan of Arc, a teenage peasant girl who felt called by God to right this egregious wrong.

Through a miraculous series of events, Joan convinced the future Charles VII to let her lead an army in his name to fight for his rightful ascension to the throne. But before leading the people into battle, Joan made a very specific request.

She asked that a banner be made for her with a painting "of Our Lord with the world in His hand"[25] and a shield with "a white dove holding in its beak a scroll."[26] And this teenage warrior insisted that these words be inscribed on the scroll: "By command of the King of Heaven."[27] Because, in the eyes of Joan of Arc, this wasn't just a battle for an earthly crown. She was fighting to eliminate injustice, which had no place in the kingdom of heaven.

Joan's example points to the first way we can scratch off the kingdom through our work: *by weeding out things in this fallen world that have no place in the eternal kingdom of God.*

As C. S. Lewis says, "The old field of space, time, matter, and the senses is to be weeded, dug, and sown for a new crop. . . . Something is being pulled down and something going up in its place."[28] That something is God's perfect and eternal reign.

This is exactly how Jesus said his kingdom would be revealed. He told his disciples, "As you go, proclaim this message: 'The kingdom of heaven has come near.' Heal the sick, raise the dead, cleanse those who have leprosy, drive out demons" (Matthew 10:7–8). In other words, heaven will be revealed by weeding out what doesn't belong in the "new crop" of the kingdom.

The apostle Paul adopted this posture of weeding as well. He understood that proclaiming the gospel doesn't just mean preaching Jesus as king. It also means exposing and confronting anything that is at odds with Jesus's kingship. In Ephesians 5:11, Paul calls all believers to expose any "deeds of darkness," and in Acts 16, we see him practicing what he preached.

The story goes like this. Paul and his companion Silas met a woman who was possessed by "a spirit by which she predicted the future" (Acts 16:16). But it wasn't just the spirit that was oppressing the woman. It was also the human traffickers who enslaved the woman who "earned a great deal of money for [them] by fortune-telling" (Acts 16:16).

This entire situation was at stark odds with the kingdom of heaven. So Paul weeded out what didn't belong in a world where Jesus is king. He drove out the spirit, leading the woman's owners to have Paul and Silas thrown into jail because they "realized that their hope of making money was gone" (Acts 16:19).

Expounding upon on this scene, one theologian says that "in the persons of Paul and Silas, two of the greatest missionaries and heroes of the faith, we see all the example we need that Christians are called to confront the economic abuses of the world."[29] And when we, like Paul, weed out anything that doesn't belong in the eternal kingdom of God, we create a thin place that allows others to glimpse what will one day be all in all.

When Joan of Arc fought against political injustice, she scratched off a glimpse of the day when the God of justice will reign supreme (see Isaiah 30:18). When you as a speech pathologist help kids weed out impediments, you're scratching off a glimpse of the day when "the stammering tongue will be fluent and clear" (Isaiah 32:4). When you as a janitor weed out literal filth, you're scratching off a glimpse of the day when God's beauty and order will abound (see Revelation 21:9–21).

Os Guinness says that "a living faith in God is the automatic refusal to accept the world as it is and a restless quest to make it what it should be under God and one day will be again."[30] That's why we weed! And that logically will lead many of us to choose to work in the darkest corners of culture, which may seem counterintuitive at first.

Let's say you work in film or politics—two industries that have long been viewed as irredeemably corrupt and sinful. As a Christian, you could be tempted to flee those industries and find a job in a church or a business led by a fellow believer— a place of work that is "better aligned with your values."

God might be calling you to do that. But he might just as well be calling you to stay exactly where you are to pull weeds in your industry that have no place in God's kingdom. After all, isn't that what Jesus himself did? Check out Hebrews 13:11–13:

> The high priest carries the blood of animals into the Most Holy Place as a sin offering, but the bodies are burned outside the camp. And so Jesus also suffered outside the city gate to make the people holy through his own blood. Let us, then, go to him outside the camp, bearing the disgrace he bore.

What does it mean that Jesus "suffered outside the city gate"? Most literally, this passage is referring to the fact that Jesus was crucified beyond Jerusalem's city walls (see John 19:17–20). But there's another meaning to this phrase.

As we saw in chapter 1, it was perfectly within God's power to have Jesus grow up working inside the city gate—in the temple. But instead, Jesus spent the majority of his life working as a tradesman "outside the city gate," where he undoubtedly suffered more blood, sweat, tears, ridicule, and temptation than the average priest. Commenting on Hebrews 13, one theologian says, "To follow Christ fully is to follow him to the places where his saving help is desperately needed, but not necessarily welcomed."[31]

Jesus isn't always welcome in much of Hollywood, Washington, D.C., Silicon Valley, and any number of other places. Which is precisely why you need to be there, believer! To weed out what doesn't align with Jesus's kingship and to scratch off glimpses of his kingdom as you do.

But it's not just weeding out what doesn't belong in eternity that reveals the kingdom. Here's the second way you and I can scratch off the kingdom through our work.

2. Plant What Does Belong in the Kingdom

To say that Nelson Mandela's twenty-seven-year imprisonment was cruel is an understatement. His seven-by-nine-foot cell could be walked in three paces.[32] He was given no bed and "only a bucket for a toilet."[33]

But perhaps the cruelest part of his incarceration was the view he was forced to endure. From his prison on Robben Island, Mandela could see Cape Town, South Africa—the beautiful city that was his rightful home. But while Mandela could see the great city, he could never step foot in it. He was able to stare at his true home but never live in it.

How did Mandela cope with the six-mile gap between his vision and his reality? He planted a garden right there in the prison yard. As he explains in his autobiography, "To plant a seed, watch it grow, to tend it and then harvest it, offered a simple but enduring satisfaction."[34]

But this garden was more than a mere distraction from the cruelty of his imprisonment. "I saw the garden as a metaphor for certain aspects of my life," Mandela says.[35] While this model of a major modern activist could no longer weed out the injustice of apartheid in South Africa, he *could* plant and "cultivate a small patch of ground to reflect the order, beauty, and abundance his soul longed for across the gap."[36]

Mandela's garden illustrates the second way you and I can reveal the kingdom through our work: *by planting foretastes of what belongs in eternity and yanking "signs and symbols" of it into the present.*[37]

We see Jesus taking this posture of revealing the kingdom throughout the Gospels. He didn't just weed out things like sickness and injustice that *don't* belong in eternity. He also planted and previewed things that *do*.

Take his first miracle as an example. When John writes about Jesus turning water into choice wine at a wedding feast, he doesn't just call the event a miracle. He calls it a "sign" (see John 2:11) because he knows that Jesus's miracle was pointing to something greater—something eternal. Jesus planted a glimpse of what Isaiah prophesies is on the other side of the veil: "a feast of rich food for all peoples, a banquet of aged wine" (Isaiah 25:6).

Jesus scratched off the kingdom by planting signs like this one in the present, and that work continues through you and me today. In 2 Corinthians 2:14, Paul says that God "uses us to spread the aroma of the knowledge of [Christ] everywhere."

When you and I create things that have the marks of the consummated kingdom, we "spread the aroma" of our King. We bring "signs and symbols of the kingdom to birth on earth as in heaven."[38]

Writers, musicians, and other creators can especially relate to this posture of scratching off the kingdom. Because as G. K. Chesterton said, "Every true artist does feel, consciously or unconsciously, that he is touching transcendental truths; that his images are shadows of things seen through the veil."[39]

Given his experience with *Phantastes,* it won't surprise you that C. S. Lewis wholeheartedly agreed. "When you painted on earth," he said, "it was because you caught glimpses of Heaven in the earthly landscape. The success of your painting was that it enabled others to see the glimpses too."[40]

But artists aren't the only ones who can plant beauty, abundance, and the other marks of the consummated kingdom. Skye Jethani encourages us to expand our thinking on this point:

> Imagine Christian educators bringing order, beauty, and abundance to schools so students and their families thrive. Imagine Christian business leaders cultivating industries that value people, pay them fairly, and steward natural resources. . . . Imagine Christian civic leaders passing just laws to ensure evil is restrained and life-giving order is possible. Such Christians would not only bring growth to our world, but they would also be cultivating the presence of [the kingdom] today.[41]

Amen. But I know some of you are still having a hard time seeing yourself in these first two postures of scratching off the kingdom. You're not weeding out injustice like a lawyer or planting glimpses of the kingdom like an artist. You work as a sales director, truck driver, or marine biologist. How can *that* work reveal the eternal kingdom of God?

3. Represent Your King

Even though Ron Johnson has one of the hardest jobs in the world—that of a customer service representative—he describes his work as "a holy calling."[42] He understands that he isn't just a representative of his company. His job offers him endless opportunities to serve as a representative of his King and to scratch off glimpses of the kingdom of God.

Johnson shares this story to illustrate: "I once spoke with a customer who was verbally abusive from the very beginning of the call. I ignored his insults . . . apologized for his inconvenience and told him what I was going to do about it. I explained how long it was going to take and promised him that, when the problem was resolved, I would call him back."[43]

Unsurprisingly, the man was skeptical of Johnson's promise.[44] But a few days later, Johnson called him to report that he had solved his problem. Johnson says, "I'll never forget his reaction when I apologized again for his inconvenience. He said, 'Well, but it gave me a chance to meet *you*. You said what you was gonna do, and you did what you said.' He sounded like he was fighting back tears."[45]

This angry customer had likely encountered countless customer service representatives in the past who were apathetic, arrogant, and incompetent. So when he encountered Johnson, who was genuinely loving, humble, and masterful at his job, the man couldn't help but get choked up. Through this ordinary call-center employee's work, the customer caught a glimpse of something transcendent and eternal.

Johnson's story shows us the third way we can scratch off glimpses of the kingdom: *by serving as faithful representatives of our King.*

While weeding and planting are more about *what* we do at work, this final posture is primarily about *how* we do the work. In the words of rapper Sho Baraka, "We are limited not by what we do but by how we do it," because "how we work will testify to the type of God we believe in."[46]

This is exactly what the apostle Paul is getting at in 2 Corinthians 5:20 when he calls us "Christ's ambassadors." Think about the role ambassadors play on behalf of nations today.* A diplomat doesn't really weed out what they perceive to be broken in the country they're posted in. And they don't really plant either. They simply serve as a representative of their home country. Their job is to be a "faithful presence" in a foreign land.[47]

Our job is largely the same. "We are called to stand in for God here in the world"—to be winsome and faithful representatives of our King and his foreign policy.[48]

When you, like Ron Johnson, work to make an angry customer happy insofar as you're able, you're scratching off a glimpse of the day when there will be perfect relationships between all people (see Revelation 7:9–17). When you work without fear in the face of great adversity, you're representing the kingdom value of peace and scratching off a glimpse of the day when anxiety will be no more (see Isaiah 32:4). When you sacrifice your freedoms for the benefit of others, you're representing the kingdom value of love and scratching off a glimpse of the day when a love supreme will reign evermore (see Revelation 22:1–5).

These everyday actions may seem insignificant compared with the Joan of Arcs of the world who are weeding out in-

---

* Or, for my fellow superfans of *The West Wing,* "ambassadors extraordinary and plenipotentiaries." God bless Lord John Marbury.

justice or the George MacDonalds and C. S. Lewises of the world who are planting glimpses of the kingdom in millions of hearts. Those heroes have had massive impact, which Andy Crouch defines as "concentrated force over a short amount of time."[49]

But while "most of us want to be a *force* . . . Jesus calls us to be a *taste*."[50] When he talked about how his kingdom would come, he didn't use the language of *impact*. He talked about "something more patient—more slow-moving but more consequential in the long run . . . something like *influence*."[51]

Take the Sermon on the Mount as an example. Jesus could have called his followers to be social crusaders or cultural elites, but instead, he called us to be "the salt of the earth" (Matthew 5:13). Salt doesn't have anything resembling impact. When used properly, it doesn't overwhelm the senses. But it does have incredible influence. It draws out, points to, and reveals the flavor of something else.

So it is with our work. Even when our jobs feel as small as a grain of salt, when we serve as faithful representatives of our King, we draw out the flavors of his kingdom. We scratch off a glimpse of what's hiding behind the thin veil between heaven and earth.

Now, I know what you might be thinking. These glimpses of the kingdom all seem so *fleeting*. Joan of Arc weeded out one instance of injustice, but millions more have popped up since. George MacDonald's novel scratched off glimpses of the kingdom, but eventually *Phantastes* will be out of print. Ron Johnson faithfully represented Christ to an angry customer, but he'll likely never talk to that person again.

In light of these sobering truths, how exactly does scratching off the kingdom matter for *eternity*? Let me offer three answers to that question before we close out this chapter.

THREE REASONS SCRATCHING OFF THE KINGDOM MATTERS FOR ETERNITY

1. God Commands It

Scripture is clear that we're called to weed out what doesn't belong in the kingdom (see Ephesians 5:11), plant what does (see 2 Corinthians 2:14–16), and rightfully represent our King (see 2 Corinthians 5:20). And every act of obedience to these commands brings God eternal pleasure and us eternal rewards, as we saw in chapters 3 and 4.

2. God May Be Using Our Advance Work to Help His Kingdom Come

In Romans 8:19–21, the apostle Paul writes,

> The creation waits in eager expectation for the children of God to be revealed. For the creation was subjected to frustration, not by its own choice, but by the will of the one who subjected it, in hope that the creation itself will be liberated from its bondage to decay and brought into the freedom and glory of the children of God.

Expounding upon this passage, N. T. Wright explains that we "are not just to be a sign and foretaste of [creation's] ultimate salvation."[52] In other words, we aren't just revealing glimpses of the kingdom here on earth. We are "part of the answer to the prayer that God's kingdom will come on earth as in heaven." Wright says, "If we pray that prayer, we shouldn't be surprised if we are called upon to help bring about God's answer to it."[53]

I once volunteered on the advance team of a presidential campaign. Days before our candidate was scheduled to arrive in New Hampshire, our team showed up at the venue to set up chairs, remove obstacles that would block people from seeing our candidate on the stage, and hand out flyers promoting the campaign event. It was only after our advance team had done our job that the candidate arrived.

In Romans 8 and elsewhere, Paul seems to be implying that our work serves a similar purpose. Much like John the Baptist did the advance work of preparing the way for Jesus's *first* coming, you and I are preparing the way for the *second* when we work to unveil his kingdom.

But even if I'm wrong and God isn't using our advance work to literally help his kingdom come, there's still a third reason our efforts to scratch off the kingdom matter for eternity.

3. Revealing the Kingdom Can Cause Others to Want to Meet Our King

You see, when we work in ways that scratch off glimpses of the kingdom of God, our work itself becomes evangelism. We have such a narrow view of evangelism that it's hard to see anything other than walking through the Romans Road fitting our definition of that term.

But God's Word makes clear that evangelism is *far* broader than tracts and street preaching. In Psalm 19, David says that "the heavens declare the glory of God" even though "they have no speech" and "use no words" (verses 1, 3). If inanimate stars trillions of miles away can "declare the glory of God," surely the work of God's image-bearers can too.

In fact, Jesus said explicitly that that's the case: "Let your light shine before others, so that they may see your good works and give glory to your Father who is in heaven" (Matthew 5:16, ESV). When your co-workers, customers, and peers "see your good works"—when they see you weeding out what doesn't belong in God's kingdom, planting what does, and faithfully representing your King—they will "give glory to your Father who is in heaven." And some will long to meet our King.

Let me offer an analogy to drive this point home. Pretend for a second that you and your friends are planning a vacation to my hometown of Tampa, Florida. As you discuss the trip, you talk about the city's gorgeous beaches, incredible Riverwalk, world-class zoo, and friendly people.

But I'm willing to bet that the mayor of Tampa *never once* comes up in your conversation. You don't travel because you're interested in the character or the policies of the person who governs a particular city. You're attracted by what that leader's policies *produce*.

I think the same is true of the kingdom of God. I think one of the primary ways that God brings people to submission to his kingship is by giving them winsome glimpses of his kingdom—the beauty, justice, peace, love, and joy that his people reveal through their lives and work.

But let's make one thing clear: Your work of weeding, planting, and representing is evangelism *even when* you don't immediately win an opportunity to explicitly share the gospel. That can be hard for us to grasp given our modern obsession with instantaneous results in everything we do. We want to plant the seed of the gospel in someone's heart and watch it blossom into full-blown faith in the same conversation. Essentially, we want to microwave people into belief in Jesus.

But that is very rarely how salvation works. The apostle Paul understood this, leading him to write these words in 1 Corinthians 3:5–6: "What, after all, is Apollos? And what is

Paul? Only servants, through whom you came to believe—as the Lord has assigned to each his task. I planted the seed, Apollos watered it, but God has been making it grow."

The Corinthians came to believe by one exposure after another to the King and his kingdom. One person planted, another watered, and Another grew their faith. So it is with us today.

"Judge each day not by the harvest you reap but by the seeds you plant."[54] And don't fall for the lie that every act of weeding, planting, and representing must be accompanied by an explicit act of evangelism. Scratching off the kingdom is intrinsically valuable to God. But as we'll see in our final chapter, it also presents unparalleled opportunities to leverage our work to the instrumental end of making disciples.

YOUR SACRED RESPONSE

In this chapter, I shared this partial list of attributes of the eternal kingdom of God:

- perfect relationship with God (see Revelation 21:3)
- perfect relationships with other people (see Psalm 46:9; Micah 4:3; Revelation 7:9–17)
- justice (see Isaiah 30:18; 61:8)
- beauty (see Isaiah 35; Revelation 21:9–21)
- order (see 1 Corinthians 14:33)
- abundance (see Isaiah 25:6–9; 49:10; 65:22; Joel 3:18)
- humility (see Matthew 19:30)
- cultural excellence (see Isaiah 60; Revelation 21:26)
- physical health (see Isaiah 32:3–4; 35:6; Revelation 21:4)
- joy (see Isaiah 65:17–18; Revelation 21:4)
- safety (see Isaiah 65:21; Ezekiel 34:28; Micah 4:4)
- sense of belonging (see Psalm 68:6)

- freedom from anxiety (see Isaiah 32:4)
- work we love to do (see Isaiah 65:22–23)
- sustainable earth (see Isaiah 51:3; Revelation 11:15–18)

Reference the list above and the questions below to help you respond practically to this chapter:

- Which of these attributes would you like to plant more of through your work?
- What might that look like practically over the next year?
- What is a single next action you can take to start to scratch off glimpses of the kingdom in this way?

You'll find space to write out your answers to these questions in *The Sacred Response* workbook, which you can download for free at jordanraynor.com/response. There you'll also find prompts for additional practices to help you scratch off the kingdom through your work, including placing a scratch-off on your desk and contextualizing "Thy kingdom come" to your workplace in prayer.

HOW TO MAKE DISCIPLES IN A
POST-CHRISTIAN WORLD WITHOUT
LEAVING TRACTS IN THE BREAK ROOM

William Wilberforce was thinking of doing the un-
thinkable: resigning his seat in the British Parliament and ending his terrifically promising political
career.

The year was 1785, and Wilberforce had just converted to
Christianity. Like many other young Christians, he now
thought the only path for serving God was quitting his "secular" job in favor of a more "sacred" one.[1]

But just to be sure, Wilberforce reached out to an old
friend and pastor named John Newton for advice. But "Newton didn't tell him what he had expected—that to follow God
he would have to leave politics. On the contrary, Newton
encouraged Wilberforce to stay where he was, saying that
God could use him there."[2]

But use him *how* exactly? Wilberforce spent nearly two
years praying and thinking through that question until he
penned this remarkable answer: He would dedicate his career
to "the suppression of the Slave Trade" throughout the British
Empire.[3]

Miraculously, God used the work of Wilberforce and many
others to accomplish just that. Days before Wilberforce's death
in 1833, the House of Commons passed a bill to free more

than eight hundred thousand African slaves.[4] Commenting on Wilberforce's extraordinary achievements, one of his many biographers says, "It's difficult to escape the verdict that William Wilberforce was simply the greatest social reformer in the history of the world."[5]

But Wilberforce wasn't just a tour de force for *social* reformation. The manumission abolitionist was also a powerful agent for *spiritual* reformation. As one biographer has noted, "Sharing [his] faith with others was central and important to Wilberforce too. And so, everywhere he went, and with everyone he met, he tried, as best he could, to bring the conversation around to the question of eternity."[6]

The results of Wilberforce's intentionality were extraordinary—almost as unbelievable as the abolition of the slave trade. "When Wilberforce entered Parliament, there were three [members of Parliament] who would have identified themselves as seriously Christian," says one historian, "but half a century later there were closer to *two hundred*."[7] And while Wilberforce was, of course, not solely responsible for this explosion of Christianity in Parliament, his biographers conclude that "Wilberforce's influence" on this revival "is hard to avoid."[8]

A TALE OF TWO DITCHES

William Wilberforce seems to have avoided the two ditches so many Christians find themselves falling into today. The first ditch is the one we've been confronting thus far in this book:

Ditch 1: Believing that the only actions of eternal significance are those that we leverage to the instrumental end of sharing the gospel

Anytime I meet someone hunkered down in this ditch, I like to point to the work of Wilberforce and ask, "Was Wilberforce's work to end slavery in the British Empire ultimately a waste of time if those freed slaves never had a chance to hear the gospel? Or would his work have been a waste had he not shared the gospel with so many in Parliament?"

The absurdity of these questions cuts to the root of the theologically flawed argument claiming that our work matters only when we leverage it to the instrumental end of carrying out the Great Commission. We know in our bones and from our Bibles that the "God of justice" (Isaiah 30:18) cares deeply about the type of work Wilberforce did *regardless* of whether the slaves' physical freedom led to spiritual freedom.

This extreme example reminds us that our work has incredible intrinsic value to God. The renowned theologian John Stott put the nail in the proverbial coffin on this point, concluding that the First Commission and the Great Commission "are independent of each other. Each stands on its own feet in its own right alongside the other. Neither is a means to the other, or even a manifestation of the other. For each is an end in itself."[9]

That truth should keep us, like Wilberforce, from falling into the first ditch. But if we're not careful, we can easily fall into an equally dangerous second ditch:

Ditch 2: Being so content with the intrinsic value of our work that we rarely, if ever, leverage our work to the instrumental end of sharing the gospel

Wilberforce clearly avoided this ditch as well. He didn't view the First Commission and the Great Commission as competing priorities. He saw them not as "either-or" but as "both-and."

The same should be true for us. Because while the first ditch is marked by a lack of faith, the second is marked by a lack of love. While leveraging our work to the instrumental end of evangelism is far from the *only* way our work matters to God, it certainly is *a* way. That brings us to the fourth way your work matters for eternity—the last that we'll explore in this book:

> **Way 4:** Your work matters for eternity because you can leverage it to the instrumental end of sharing the gospel with those you work with.

If at times in this book I've come across as too harsh with those who argue that the Great Commission is the only commission, it's only because I'm trying to compensate for decades of unbiblical indoctrination you and I have endured that assigns zero intrinsic value to our work. But the risk, of course, is swinging the pendulum too far in the opposite direction.

Can I be real for a second? I almost didn't write this book because I feared it might make you less engaged in the Great Commission. And if I've done that, then I've failed. But I'm confident that won't be the case.

As I mentioned in the introduction of this book, in my experience, it's the people who most deeply understand the intrinsic value of their work that are most effective at leveraging their work to the instrumental end of evangelism. Why? Because when you know that God cares about 100 percent of the time you spend at work and not just the 1 percent when you get to explicitly share the gospel, *it makes you come fully alive.* And fully alive people attract the lost like honey attracts bees, giving us an endless stream of opportunities to boldly proclaim the hope we have in Christ.

But just to be sure you don't close this book less committed to sharing the gospel than when you started it, let me quickly spell out three truths to help us all avoid falling into the second ditch.

THREE TRUTHS TO ENSURE YOU FULLY EMBRACE THE GREAT COMMISSION

1. Your Salvation Has Made You a Debtor

In Romans 1:14–15, Paul writes, "I am a debtor . . . both to wise and to unwise. So, as much as is in me, I am ready to preach the gospel to you" (NKJV). Paul is saying that God's free gift of salvation should lead not just to feelings of *gratitude* but also to a sense of *indebtedness* to share that gift with others. Not to earn our salvation, but in response to it.

Here's the sobering truth: Some, perhaps even most, of your co-workers will likely spend eternity without God. That should grieve us and scare the hell out of them.

Now, I *hate* "turn or burn" preaching as much as I'm sure you do, but there's something to be said for the fact that while Jesus was constantly telling his followers *not* to fear things like hunger, storms, and physical death (see Matthew 6:25; Mark 4:35–41; 5:35–36), he frequently *encouraged* them to fear eternity without God. And he used terrifying and graphic language about hell to do so (see Matthew 13:42, 49–50; 18:9; 25:30, 41; Mark 9:43–48; Luke 16:19–31).

It's clear that the one thing Jesus *wants* us to fear is eternal separation from him. That fear should produce in us a healthy sense of urgency to share the gospel with those we work with.

Here's the second truth to keep in mind if you find yourself failing to leverage your work to the instrumental end of evangelism.

2. The Great Commission Isn't Primarily for Those Who "Go" to All Nations

Matthew 28:19 records Jesus telling his followers, "Go and make disciples of all nations." These are some of the most famous and misinterpreted words in all of Scripture. For years, I interpreted this verse as meaning that if I *really* loved Jesus, I would be a missionary living in poverty and squalor in a jungle thousands of miles away from home—not working as an entrepreneur in sunny Tampa, Florida.

But my understanding of the Great Commission radically changed when I heard the brilliant Dr. Kennon Vaughan explain the literal meaning of the Greek word *poreuthentes*, which we translate as "Go" in "Go and make disciples." Vaughan says,

> The word "Go" literally means "having gone." "Go" is not a command. [Jesus] is not commanding them to go, as much as he is saying, "Having gone . . . turn men into disciples!" . . . The going is assumed. . . . Jesus didn't go more than two hundred miles away from his own hometown, and yet he is saying go make disciples of all nations. . . . It wasn't about how far he went. It was about what he did while he was going. The same is true for you.[10]

Assuming that you've already gone, make disciples. That changes everything, doesn't it? The Great Commission isn't something we do only on a short-term missions trip or when we enter the "halftime" of our career and take a job at a church or ministry.[11] It's part of how we do what we do all our lives.

And oh, by the way, you're currently in an *ideal* position to make disciples, which brings me to the final truth that should inspire us to embrace the instrumental value of our work.

3. Mere Christians—Not Full-Time Missionaries—Are Usually the Most Effective at Making Disciples

I mentioned this in the introduction of the book, but it's such a mind-blowing statistic that it bears repeating here: "80% or more of evangelism in the early church was done not by ministers or evangelists" but by mere Christians like you and me![12]

Dr. Michael Green, an expert on the explosion of Christianity in the first few centuries, says that the historical evidence "makes it abundantly clear that in contrast to the present day, when Christianity is . . . dispensed by a professional clergy . . . in the early days the faith was spontaneously spread by informal evangelists," who shared the gospel "in homes and wine shops, on walks, and around market stalls."[13]

Which is why the apostle Paul *chose* to work as a tentmaker rather than a donor-supported missionary (see 1 Corinthians 9:14–23)! Paul knew that it was through tentmakers and shepherds, not primarily through pastors and other religious professionals, that the gospel would spread.

Jesus knew this, too, of course. His model of ministry wasn't to build a church and pray that people came. When he kicked off his kingdom-building project, his proverbial business card read "carpenter," not "preacher." And when he recruited others to proclaim the gospel of the kingdom, he didn't call the Pharisees and other religious professionals of the day. He called fishermen and tax collectors!

Since the beginning, Christianity has spread most rapidly through mere Christians embracing the Great Commission *as they go about* fulfilling the First Commission to fill, subdue, and rule this world for God's glory. And that's likely going to be true for the foreseeable future.

Why? Because the fastest-growing religious affiliation is *no* religious affiliation![14] Non-Christians are less likely than ever to step inside a church to learn about Jesus. So where will they hear the good news? *Through you and me* working shoulder to shoulder with them Monday through Friday.

The question, then, is, How can we do the work of the Great Commission well in our increasingly post-Christian culture? We know that street preaching in front of our offices and adding John 3:16 to our Zoom backgrounds isn't going to cut it. So what will?

Over the years, I've explored that question with hundreds of people on my podcast and in my community. Here are the seven things that come up over and over again.

HOW TO BEST POSITION YOURSELF TO MAKE DISCIPLES AT WORK

1. Pray

Every morning before she walks into the school, lunch lady Jillian Jenkins sits in her car and prays. "I pray that I will be the light of Jesus," she tells me. "I pray that I'll serve the way Jesus serves. And I pray for the salvation of my students."[15]

It can be tempting to think that it's up to us to pry open doors to share the gospel with those we work with. But Jenkins knows that it's God alone who can make people receptive to his good news. Which is why she, like the apostle Paul, prays "that God may open a door for our message, so that we may proclaim the mystery of Christ" (Colossians 4:3).

We must do the same. If we want to see our co-workers

come to faith in Christ, we must begin by praying for their salvation.

But we can't *just* pray. We can't "let go and let God," because 2 Corinthians 5:20 says that God is "making his appeal [to nonbelievers] through *us.*" Which brings me to the second thing we need to do to position ourselves to make disciples at work.

2. Be So Good They Can't Ignore You

Steve Jobs was in Hawaii when he pulled out his iPhone to call Ron Johnson. Not to be confused with the customer service representative we met in chapter 5, this Ron Johnson was the person Jobs chose to help him create the Apple Store.

Johnson and Jobs had shared hundreds of phone calls over the years, but this one would prove to be monumental. Jobs had discovered that he had been diagnosed with cancer, and he was calling to discuss the news with his friend.

Eventually, Jobs said, "Ron, you teach Sunday school, right?"

"Yeah," Johnson replied.

"Tell me about your faith," Jobs said.

And right then and there, Johnson shared the gospel with his friend.[16]

But here's the thing: Johnson would have never had the opportunity to share the gospel with Jobs had he not been exceptional at his craft. It was Johnson's extraordinary work on the Apple Store that won him Jobs's respect, his friendship, and an opportunity to share his faith in his friend's darkest hour.

Johnson's example shows us the second way we can best position ourselves to make disciples at work: In the words of comedian Steve Martin, "Be so good they can't ignore you."[17]

I think this is part of what the apostle Paul is getting at in 1 Thessalonians 4:11–12 when he says, "You should mind your own business and work with your hands, just as we told you, so that your daily life may win the respect of outsiders." In 2 Corinthians 6:3–5, he goes even further, saying that we must engage in excellent "hard work" so that our witness "will not be discredited."

Those are strong words, but Paul, of course, is exactly right. Mediocrity doesn't "win the respect of outsiders." *Mastery* does. My friend Andrew Scott says that "if we were to live out our lives with excellence for the purposes of God in every sector of society, we would not have to shout so loudly to make our message heard."[18]

Amen. But it's not just technical excellence that positions us to share the gospel with those we work with. It's also friendship.

3. Be a Friend

When Williams Mahlangu joined the human resources team at his South African firm, he went out of his way to learn the names and stories of everyone in his department. Why? Because "it speaks volumes when you value people not because of their role, but because of who God created them to be," he says.[19]

And sure enough, it has been Mahlangu's simple acts of friendship that "God [has] used . . . to open doors" to share the gospel.[20] "I think they saw (Jesus) in me," Mahlangu says. "And because they fell in love with Him, they gave me favor."[21]

Being a friend. Who knew? Well, Jesus for one. In John 13:34–35, he said, "As I have loved you, so you must love one another. *By this* everyone will know that you are my disciples."

Our co-workers won't know we are Christians if we work only with excellence. They will know we are Christians if we work with excellence *and* love.*

In addition to being known as exceptional professionals, we need to be known as exceptional people—ones who genuinely love those they work with and not just the product of their work. Here are a few examples of what this could look like practically:

- Pick up your friend's favorite Starbucks drink for them on your way into work.
- Praise your friend in front of your other co-workers.
- Donate a vacation or sick day to a friend who's struggling with an illness or caring for a sick loved one.
- Take a meal to a new parent, who (take it from me) won't have the time or energy to cook a good meal for years.
- Invite one of your co-workers who's alone for a holiday to celebrate with you.†

Being a friend is simple, but it's not easy. It requires that we sacrifice time, energy, and money. But it's more than worth it when God uses our love to soften people's hearts toward him.

But being a friend isn't enough.

There's an old adage attributed to Saint Francis of Assisi: "Preach the gospel always; if necessary, use words." While I appreciate the sentiment, this quote is ridiculous. Actions

---

* Although to be clear, excellence *is* a form of love. More on the ministry of excellence in chapter 3 of my book *Master of One*.

† Want more practical ideas on how to be a great friend to those you work with? I've shared more in *The Sacred Response* workbook, which you can download for free at jordanraynor.com/response.

aren't enough. At some point, we have to speak up about our allegiance to Christ, which brings me to the fourth thing we need to do to best position ourselves to make disciples at work.

4. Identify Yourself as a Christian

A missionary traveled to Saudi Arabia, where she planned to stay in the home of some Muslim friends. She was stunned by what she found when she went downstairs one day during her visit: Eighty people were waiting to hear her teach about Jesus.[22]

The missionary turned to her host and asked, "Isn't that illegal in Saudi Arabia? How has this come about?"[23]

The host said, "I have a Filipino housemaid. She sings all the time and looks so joyful. I asked her what she was singing about, and she explained she was singing songs of praise and thanksgiving to God for Jesus."[24]

According to the leader of one of the world's largest missions agencies, domestic workers like this maid "have done more for the spread of the gospel in the Arabian Peninsula *than all the traditional missionaries put together.*"[25] But that extraordinary result would be impossible without the courage of people like this Filipino woman who publicly identify themselves as Christians.

We can't just pray for the salvation of our co-workers and do our work with excellence and love. If we want to make disciples of Jesus Christ, at some point we have to raise our hands and say that we are disciples of Jesus Christ.

This can be a scary and awkward thing to do, which is why I think many Christians treat Jesus the way teenagers treat their parents while in public: never quite denying them, but walking so far behind that there's no way anyone would mistake them as being together.[26]

The consequences for treating Jesus in this way are grave. He said, "Whoever acknowledges me before others, I will also acknowledge before my Father in heaven. But whoever disowns me before others, I will disown before my Father in heaven" (Matthew 10:32–33).

Now, Jesus is *not* saying that you can lose your salvation if you don't acknowledge him at work (see John 10:28–29; Romans 8:38–39). But if you've never publicly identified yourself as a Christian, it may be a sign that you were never saved in the first place (see Romans 10:9). "God wants no faint hearts for his ambassadors."[27] He wants followers who will boldly declare their allegiance to him.

But what does this look like practically? Because I don't think most of us can get away with singing hymns in our offices like the Filipino maid. So how can we identify ourselves as Christians in a natural, nonthreatening way that doesn't cause our co-workers to avoid making eye contact with us? Let me suggest five simple ideas that have worked well for me and others:

1. *Ask about your co-workers' weekend.* And when they inevitably ask about your weekend, tell them about the time of worship you participated in at your church.
2. *Ask what your colleagues are reading.* And again, when they reciprocate the question, talk about a book you've recently read about the Christian faith.
3. *Tell a co-worker that you've prayed for them.* Nobody gets mad about someone praying on their behalf.
4. *Add something about your faith to your social media bios.* You'd be shocked at how many doors this simple practice has opened for me to talk about my faith.
5. *Encourage your team to bring their whole selves to work.* There's a trend in business these days that encourages

employees to bring their whole selves to work—their sexual identity, stories about their family, their religious beliefs, their political leanings, etc. If you're in a position of authority in your workplace, lean into this trend! Encourage those who work with you to talk openly about these things. Not only can this lead to higher productivity, but it also gives you an opportunity to identify yourself as a Christ-follower and learn about the spiritual beliefs of those you work with.[28]

None of these actions in and of themselves are likely to lead someone to faith in Christ. But each can provide a critical step in that direction because nobody is going to ask you why you follow Jesus until you make it clear that you follow Jesus.

But here's the thing: We don't need to be exclusively reactive and always waiting for others to bring conversations around to Christianity. There are also ways to proactively steer conversations in that direction.

5. Look for Opportunities to Move from the Surface, to the Serious, to the Spiritual

By default, the conversations we have with our co-workers tend to be largely superficial. We talk about sports, the weather, and our plans for the weekend. But I've found that, with just a little bit of intentionality (and a lot of God's grace), it's easy to steer conversations from the surface, to the serious, to the spiritual.[29]

Let me share an example. When I served as the CEO of a large tech start-up, I struck up a conversation with a colleague I'll call Jen. Our conversation started on the surface with me asking Jen how her kids' soccer game went on Saturday. "It was so much fun," she said, "but I was just *so* exhausted from last week."

Sensing an opportunity to move from the surface to the serious, I said, "Yeah, I've noticed you've been working *super* late the past few weeks. I'm curious to know why. You know I don't require that of you, right?"

Jen said, "Well, I love this job! But I think I work so hard because I grew up pretty poor. And so I guess I've always seen my career as a way of proving I'm more successful than my parents."

Now we were moving from the serious to the spiritual. I told Jen, "I've been there! For a long time, I used my work to prove something to my parents and my friends. But a few years ago, I realized that no amount of success was ever going to be enough. I know it might sound weird, but it was my faith that got me off that exhausting hamster wheel."

Of course, the dialogue wasn't that polished, but that was the gist of the conversation. And by God's grace, it opened up an opportunity to share the gospel with Jen.

Simply keeping this "surface, serious, spiritual" framework in mind as you talk with your co-workers can be enormously helpful, as it gives you a mental map to spot where you are and where you want to take a conversation. But if you want to be even more proactive, then let me encourage you to adopt the simple but *ingenious* practice that enabled William Wilberforce to be the disciple-making juggernaut you read about at the beginning of this chapter.

For much of his life, Wilberforce made lists of what he called "launchers"—"subjects he could bring up with each friend that might launch them into a conversation about spiritual issues."[30] Here are a few examples straight from one of Wilberforce's lists:

S—— *and Mrs.* What books reading? To give them good ones—Walker's Sermons. . . . Education of their children, to inquire about. . . . Their coming some Sunday to Battersea Rise to hear Venn.

V——. Try what he believes and speak home truths.

Sir R. Has he read Doddridge?[31]

So simple but *so* crazy brilliant. Did all of these launchers succeed in moving conversations from the surface, to the serious, to the spiritual? Of course not. "Wilberforce . . . had many disappointments, frankly chronicled in [his] diary."[32] But many of his launchers *did* work, so he made drafting them a lifelong habit.

I've found this practice to be so helpful that I've made it a part of my own efforts to share the gospel with the non-Christians I know. Instead of making a list on paper like Wilberforce, I've created a simple Google Doc named "Launchers" that I can access wherever. Here are a few examples of the launchers on my list:

- Brian (a lapsed Catholic): What are your kids' favorite Christmas traditions? → Did you grow up going to Christmas Eve Mass? → Would you guys want to come to church with Kara, the kids, and me on Christmas Eve?
- Mark (an agnostic): Text him to schedule lunch → Discuss the book I read per his recommendation → Give him a copy of *The Reason for God* given his interest in thought-provoking books about spirituality
- Lisa (grew up in the church but fell away): Last time we talked, you mentioned a church you went to in college.

What denomination was it? → Why did you stop going to church after college?*

Moments before I expect to see these friends, I'll quickly pull open my "Launchers" doc on my phone and review my notes for that person. More often than not, I've seen God use launchers like these to move conversations from the surface, to the serious, to the spiritual. I'm confident you will too.

Okay, there are two more things we need to do to prepare to make the most of the conversations our launchers lead us into.

6. Be Prepared to Give a Reason for Your Faith

By God's grace, I was able to move my conversation with Jen from the surface, to the serious, to the spiritual. But I would have never had an opportunity to explicitly share the gospel with her had I not been prepared to share the reason I don't work all hours of the day like she did—namely, my faith in Christ and not my professional success.

If you've tackled numbers 1–5 on this list, eventually somebody is going to ask you . . .

- "Why do you never respond to emails on Sundays?"
- "What is this small group I keep hearing you talk about?"
- "You don't seem nearly as anxious as the rest of our team. Why?"
- "Why did you and your husband adopt instead of having another child biologically?"
- "My mom is dying, and I know you're religious: What do you believe about the afterlife?"

* Names have been changed to protect the innocent.

The apostle Peter said that before those questions are ever asked, we are to "be prepared to give an answer to everyone who asks you to give the reason for the hope that you have" (1 Peter 3:15). That's the question underneath all the questions above, isn't it? *What is the source of your hope?*

If we want to leverage our work to the instrumental end of sharing the gospel, we've got to be prepared to answer that question in the many forms it takes. We must be able to articulate why we believe what we believe on two levels.

First, *we must be prepared to share the personal reasons for our faith.*

This is, in essence, your testimony—the story of how God has changed your life, which nobody can dispute. When I told Jen that Christ alone got me off the exhausting hamster wheel of always needing more success to feel worthy, I was giving her a personal reason for the hope that I have.

But personal reasons go only so far. Which is why *we must also be prepared to share the universal reasons for our faith*—the intellectual and historical case for our hope.

Many of your co-workers likely view Christianity as lacking intellectual rigor. But you and I know that our faith is *far* from a blind one. It's built on heaps of historical evidence and logical arguments. But if we can't articulate those things, we're going to have a hard time leading our co-workers to Christ.

Now, I know this task sounds *incredibly* intimidating, which is why I've created a list of my favorite resources to help you prepare to share the universal reasons for your faith. You can find it in *The Sacred Response* workbook at jordanraynor.com/response.

Once you're prepared to give a reason for your faith, there's only one thing left to do to position yourself to make disciples at work.

7. *Be Prepared to Clear Your Calendar*

When I'm on my morning runs, I often run into neighbors who are on my list of launchers. If it's clear that they're in the mood to chat (and I don't have a Zoom meeting forcing me to get back to my home office by a certain time), I will often stop to talk—and I mentally clear my calendar.

Not because the work that's waiting for me at my desk doesn't matter to God! Everything we've seen in this book tells us that it does. I clear my calendar because I know that opportunities to converse with nonbelievers are incredibly rare and fleeting.

If you want to make disciples at work, you should be prepared to do the same—making time and space on your calendar to talk with those who are ready to go from the surface to the serious to the spiritual.

But a word of caution is in order for the majority of you who work for someone else. Immediately after Peter told his readers, "Be prepared to . . . give the reason for the hope that you have," he said, "But do this with gentleness and respect" (1 Peter 3:15). Of course, this means showing respect to the person we're sharing the gospel with, but we're also called to show respect to our employers!

Your company pays you to do a job, and I'm willing to bet that sharing the gospel isn't a part of your job description. You could make an argument that sharing the gospel with a co-worker during normal business hours is stealing from your employer, which, of course, thwarts your witness to them (see Titus 2:9–10).

That means we need to prayerfully consider when and where we share the gospel with those we work with, as we're called to obey the Great Commission *and* Scripture's repeated command that we serve our employers with excellence as we go about the First Commission (see Ephesians 6:5–8; Colossians 3:22–25).

But make the time we must, because making disciples in our virtual and physical offices is clearly one of the ways our "labor in the Lord is not in vain" (1 Corinthians 15:58).

YOUR SACRED RESPONSE

Before you turn to the short epilogue that concludes this book, take action on what you just read by building your own list of launchers.

This is *by far* the most effective practice I've found for moving conversations with co-workers from the surface, to the serious, to the spiritual. And it's super simple to start.

- *Step 1:* Choose a place where you'll keep your list of launchers. This could be a physical journal, a note on your phone, a Google Doc—whatever.
- *Step 2:* Make a list of people you want to be intentional about sharing the gospel with at work.
- *Step 3:* Next to each person's name, list a few questions and/or topics that you think would lead a conversation with them from the surface, to the serious, to the spiritual.

Need some inspiration on that third step? I've shared some examples of launchers that have worked well for me and others in *The Sacred Response* workbook, which you can download for free at jordanraynor.com/response. There you'll find a link to a Google Doc and PDF template that you can copy and customize.

The workbook also includes a bunch more practices to

help you make disciples through your work, including the Keeper Test to determine if you're so good they can't ignore you (this one alone can change your life and career), picking a strategy for outing yourself as a Christian, and documenting your personal reasons for your faith.

EPILOGUE

Make It Matter More

Sixto Rodriguez was the biggest rock star you've never heard of—unless you grew up in South Africa, that is. Because it was there and there alone that, in the 1970s and '80s, Rodriguez was "bigger than the Beatles, bigger than the Rolling Stones, bigger than Elvis Presley."[1]

But get this: For twenty-five years, Rodriguez *had no idea* of his fame. While an entire nation was singing his songs, he was fighting to earn a living wage for his family in Detroit.

The story goes like this. In 1968, Rodriguez walked into a studio to record an album called *Cold Fact* alongside the best of the best in the music business—a team who produced A-list artists like Michael Jackson, Stevie Wonder, and Ringo Starr.

But even with that crazy pedigree, these producers saw something special in this young Mexican American song-writer. As one member of his team put it, "Bob Dylan was *mild* [compared] to *this* guy."[2]

Needless to say, expectations for Rodriguez's debut album were sky high. But when *Cold Fact* was released in the United States, it totally, utterly bombed. When the head of Rodriguez's record label was asked to estimate how many copies *Cold Fact* sold, he replied, "In America? Six"—clearly only slightly exaggerating.[3]

When Rodriguez's sophomore album suffered the same fate a year later, he gave up on his rock-star dreams and spent the next twenty-five years doing hard manual labor such as demolition and painting—what one of his friends described as "dirty, dirty work."[4]

And while Rodriguez genuinely enjoyed the work, it was barely enough to make ends meet. He was forced to move his daughters into twenty-six different homes around Detroit, all without knowing that, at the exact same time, many of South Africa's twenty-six million citizens were in *their* homes playing his records.

Apparently, one of the "six" Americans who bought *Cold Fact* carried the album on a plane to South Africa. And when she played the record for her friends, they all began clamoring for their own copies. The only problem was that *Cold Fact* wasn't for sale in South Africa, so these new fans started bootlegging the record.

Soon the album was *everywhere*. As one South African record store owner explained, "To us, it was one of the most famous records of all time."[5]

But Rodriguez had no clue. After *Cold Fact* started to explode, a South African record label began distributing the album in partnership with Rodriguez's label in the States. But somehow (quite suspiciously) his royalties got lost in the mail, leaving him blind to his influence.[6]

Just as Rodriguez was in the dark about his fame, South Africans were in the dark about Rodriguez's identity. Nobody knew anything about their favorite rock star, leading most to accept a widely peddled myth that Rodriguez had committed suicide onstage in America.

But that story was hard for some fans to accept, including journalist Craig Strydom. So in the mid-1990s, Strydom organized a team to go searching for Rodriguez—a wild story, brilliantly captured in the Oscar-winning documentary *Searching for Sugar Man*. And sure enough, in 1997, these South African fans found Rodriguez very much alive in Detroit.

The call that finally connected these two previously disconnected worlds took place around 8:00 P.M. eastern time, at the end of another hard day of work for Rodriguez. When he lifted the phone to his ear, he couldn't believe what he heard.

"You're bigger than Elvis," the South African told him.

Rodriguez replied, "What do you mean?"

"In South Africa, you are more popular than Elvis Presley."[7]

And then there was a long pause. The news was truly unbelievable. For years, Rodriguez was convinced his music had been ignored, forgotten, *totally* in vain. But on the other end of the phone, a new friend was assuring him that his work was having an extraordinary impact in a distant, unseen land.

My prayer is that this book has metaphorically served as that phone call for you, believer, helping you see the incredible impact your work is already having in the seemingly distant, unseen dimension of heaven. Your job that others call "secular" is anything but. The years you've spent working "as for the Lord" have not been for naught (Colossians 3:23, ESV). *None* of "your labor in the Lord" has been in vain (1 Corinthians 15:58).

I hope that truth has been *massively* encouraging to you as you've read this book. But my prayer is also that it would challenge you to make your work matter more. Because while all good, God-honoring work matters for eternity, not all work matters *equally* for eternity. And since today is a rounding error in the grand scheme of eternity, the most rational thing you can do is optimize this life for the next one. To spend it, rather than save it. To take every opportunity you can to make your work matter even *more* for eternity.

That could look like being more intentional about doing your work *with* God and not just *for* him, as a means of bringing him greater eternal pleasure as we saw in chapter 3.

It could look like continuing to work on your magnum opus while showing mercy to your neighbors, thus increasing the chances that your work is rewarded with the distinction of the glory of the nations as we saw in chapter 4.

Maybe God is calling you to fully fund adoptions for your team members as a means of scratching off glimpses of the justice and belonging that are offered to every citizen of the kingdom of heaven as we saw in chapter 5.

Or maybe God is leading you to build a list of launchers and get serious about making disciples while you go about your current work as we saw in chapter 6.

Whatever it is, *please* don't close this book without responding to its truths. To riff off the theological giant Spider-Man, with great knowledge comes great responsibility. Now that you know your work matters for eternity, your responsibility is to make it matter more. Not for your glory, but for God's. Not to earn your salvation, but as a response to it (see Ephesians 2:8–10).

There's a beautiful picture of this in the life of Rodriguez. After he learned of the impact his work was having in South Africa, he began making plans to perform in the country that had made him a star.

The moment Rodriguez walked onto that stage in Cape Town is one of the most remarkable I've ever seen on film. I dare you to watch it without crying. For almost ten minutes, his voice was drowned out by the rapturous applause of tens of thousands of fans. All because he chose not just to be encouraged by that momentous phone call but to *do* something about it. To make his work matter even more in that foreign land.

I pray that you will have a similar response to *The Sacredness of Secular Work*. I pray that you will put this book down encouraged and challenged to make your work matter even more in the kingdom of heaven—not for the applause of others on this side of the veil, but for the applause of the One you will bow before on the other side.

ACKNOWLEDGMENTS

To my fellow mere Christians: Whether you know it or not, *you* dictate what I make next, and this book is a result of your over-the-top enthusiasm for the themes herein. Thank you for your nonstop encouragement and for sharing my work with the world!

To my bride, Kara: I've said it once, and I will say it again—thank you for graciously letting me complain that "I'm nowhere" at the start of this and every other book. And thank you for the extraordinary work you do that allows me to focus on this work.

To my daughters, Ellison, Kate, and Emery: Thank you for helping me pick the cover for this book. And for stopping me from titling it *Not in Vain*. I love you more than you will ever be able to comprehend!

To my assistant, Kayla: You're the most tenured employee I've ever had for a reason. Thank you for being exceptional at what you do.

To my agent, D. J. Snell: Five years ago, I was thrilled that we got to do *one* book together, and now six?! It has truly been my privilege. You are the best of the best.

To my editor, Estee Zandee: You made this *such* a better book. Thank you for reminding me of the best note I've ever received: "Look the reader in the eye." And thank you for putting up with my *insane* obsession over every word and parenthesis my team tests in book titles.

To the rest of the team at WaterBrook: Thank you for your partnership over these five books and for your dedication to filling the earth with the glory of the nations.

To the many friends who encouraged me in the midst of this project: Chris Adams, Tim Keller, John Mark Comer, Cheryl Bachelder, Skye Jethani, Jenna Barrett, Jon Houghton, JP Pokluda, Andrew Scott and the team at OM, Michael Thompson and the team at Turas, David Roth and the team at Workmatters, and many others. I don't think I would have written this book without your words of affirmation.

To those who provided feedback on the first draft: Chris Basham, Mark Batterson, Dave Hataj, Chassie Anders, Chris Griffin, Daniel Vos, Kaleigh Cox, and many more. You made this a much more nuanced and empathetic book.

To those who did the hard theological work that my readers and I now benefit from: N. T. Wright, Randy Alcorn, Darrell Cosden, Sandra Richter, Makoto Fujimura, James Davison Hunter, Richard Mouw, Hugh Whelchel, Robbie Castleman, R. Paul Stevens, Amy Sherman, and the team at the Theology of Work Project. This book wouldn't exist without you all.

To Jonathan and the team at Elevation: I can't tell you how many times a twelve-ounce drip with steamed almond milk and two stevias helped me push through a tough section of this book. Thank you!

To Taylor and Lin: There's no one who can match you for turn of phrase. Thank you for giving me more Easter eggs than I could have ever expected in my wildest dreams.

To the Church at Odessa: Your support of my work means

so much because you know me (the good and the bad) so well. I love you all.

To my heavenly Father: "If you had not loved me first, I would refuse you still."[1] Thank you for the miracle of my salvation and for inviting me to work *with* you and *for* you for eternity. *Soli Deo gloria.*

NOTES

INTRODUCTION: WHAT IF THE GREAT COMMISSION *ISN'T* WHAT IT'S ALL ABOUT?

1. Hunter Baker, "Charitable Choice and Secular Goods," Acton Institute, February 25, 2009, www.acton.org/pub/commentary /2009/02/25/charitable-choice-and-secular-goods.
2. Charles Spurgeon, "All for Jesus!" (sermon, Metropolitan Tabernacle, London, November 29, 1874), www.spurgeongems.org /sermon/chs1205.pdf.
3. Lisa Miller, "Pope's Book: A Lifetime of Learning," *Newsweek,* May 20, 2007, www.newsweek.com/popes-book-lifetime -learning-101009.
4. N. T. Wright, *Surprised by Hope: Rethinking Heaven, the Resurrection, and the Mission of the Church* (New York: HarperOne, 2008), 193.
5. Amy L. Sherman, *Kingdom Calling: Vocational Stewardship for the Common Good* (Downers Grove, Ill.: IVP Books, 2011), 104.
6. I've got to give credit where credit is due: Thank you, Tom Nelson, for these helpful terms. Tom Nelson, *Work Matters: Connecting Sunday Worship to Monday Work* (Wheaton, Ill.: Crossway, 2011), 60.
7. Rick Warren, *The Purpose Driven Life: What on Earth Am I Here For?*, rev. ed. (Grand Rapids, Mich.: Zondervan, 2012), 282.
8. Jen Wilkin, *None like Him: 10 Ways God Is Different from Us (and Why That's a Good Thing)* (Wheaton, Ill.: Crossway, 2016), 79, emphasis added.

9. John Mark Comer, *Garden City: Work, Rest, and the Art of Being Human* (Grand Rapids, Mich.: Zondervan, 2015), 107.

10. Robbie F. Castleman, "The Last Word: The Great Commission; Ecclesiology," *Themelios* 32, no. 3 (2007): 68, www.thegospel coalition.org/themelios/article/the-last-word-the-great -commission-ecclesiology.

11. Daniel L. Akin, Benjamin L. Merkle, and George G. Robinson, *40 Questions About the Great Commission* (Grand Rapids, Mich.: Kregel Academic, 2020), 64, emphasis added.

12. Preface to *The Holy Bible, New International Version* (Grand Rapids, Mich.: Zondervan, 2011), www.bible-researcher.com /niv2011-preface.html.

13. Mathew Schmalz, "What Is the Great Commission and Why Is It So Controversial?," The Conversation, February 8, 2019, https://theconversation.com/what-is-the-great-commission-and -why-is-it-so-controversial-111138.

14. Often attributed to J. Hudson Taylor, but no original source has been located.

15. Andrew Scott, "Andrew Scott (CEO of Operation Mobilization USA)," interview by Jordan Raynor, *Mere Christians,* podcast, 44:39, June 29, 2022, https://podcast.jordanraynor.com /episodes/andrew-scott-ceo-of-operation-mobilization-usa.

16. Chris Basham, email message to author, January 18, 2023.

17. Dan Foster, "What Jesus Actually Said," *Backyard Church,* October 12, 2020, https://medium.com/backyard-theology/what -jesus-actually-said-8b4bbb0a50e8.

18. Randy Alcorn, *Heaven* (Carol Stream, Ill.: Tyndale Momentum, 2004), 125.

19. Often attributed to Oliver Wendell Holmes, but no original source has been located.

20. N. T. Wright, *Acts for Everyone, Part 1: Chapters 1–12* (Louisville, Ky.: Westminster John Knox, 2008), 86.

21. Timothy Keller, *How to Reach the West Again: Six Essential Elements of a Missionary Encounter* (New York: Redeemer City to City, 2020), 18.

22. "In U.S., Decline of Christianity Continues at Rapid Pace,"

Pew Research Center, October 17, 2019, www.pewresearch.org
/religion/2019/10/17/in-u-s-decline-of-christianity-continues
-at-rapid-pace.

23. Andrew Scott, *Scatter: Go Therefore and Take Your Job with You* (Chicago: Moody, 2016), 153.

24. Skye Jethani, *Futureville: Discover Your Purpose for Today by Reimagining Tomorrow* (Nashville, Tenn.: Nelson Books, 2013), 107–8.

25. Lin-Manuel Miranda, "The Room Where It Happens," *Hamilton,* directed by Thomas Kail (Burbank, Calif.: Walt Disney Studios Motion Pictures, 2020), Disney+.

26. Leo Tolstoy, *A Confession and Other Religious Writings,* trans. Jane Kentish (London: Penguin, 1987), 34–35.

27. Dorothy L. Sayers, "Why Work?," in *Letters to a Diminished Church: Passionate Arguments for the Relevance of Christian Doctrine* (Nashville, Tenn.: Thomas Nelson, 2004), 130.

CHAPTER 1: THE UNABRIDGED GOSPEL

1. "About Human Trafficking," U.S. Department of State, www
.state.gov/humantrafficking-about-human-trafficking.

2. Human Trafficking Institute, "The Problem," https://trafficking
institute.org/why-trafficking.

3. This statistic was calculated by comparing the 2019 and 2020 Trafficking in Persons Reports: "2019 Trafficking in Persons Report," June 2019, www.state.gov/reports/2019-trafficking-in -persons-report; "2020 Trafficking in Persons Report," June 2020, www.state.gov/reports/2020-trafficking-in-persons -report.

4. David Green with Bill High, *Leadership Not by the Book: 12 Unconventional Principles to Drive Incredible Results* (Grand Rapids, Mich.: Baker Books, 2022), 73.

5. "For Kids," The Gospel Project, Lifeway, accessed December 7, 2022, https://gospelproject.lifeway.com/kids.

6. Rick Warren, *The Purpose Driven Life: What on Earth Am I Here For?,* rev. ed. (Grand Rapids, Mich.: Zondervan, 2012), 99, emphasis added.

7. *New Testament,* Museum of the Bible, Washington, D.C., January 15, 2022.

8. Timothy Keller, *Ministries of Mercy: The Call of the Jericho Road,* 3rd ed. (Phillipsburg, N.J.: P&R, 2015), 31.

9. Frost Smith, "Evolution and What the Image of God Is Not," Answers in Genesis, August 8, 2015, https://answersingenesis.org /are-humans-animals/evolution-and-what-image-god-is-not.

10. Tim Keller, "The Gospel—Key to Change," *Cru Press Green,* accessed January 25, 2023, www.cru.org/content/dam/cru /legacy/2013/01/Gospel_KeytoChange_TimKeller.pdf.

11. Michael Metzger, "The Widest Story Ever Told," Clapham Institute, October 12, 2020, https://claphaminstitute.org/the -widest-story-ever-told.

12. Michael Metzger, "Back and Forth," Clapham Institute, January 19, 2007, https://claphaminstitute.org/back-and-forth.

13. Warren, *Purpose Driven Life,* 99, emphasis added.

14. Alasdair MacIntyre, *After Virtue: A Study in Moral Theory,* 3rd ed. (Notre Dame, Ind.: University of Notre Dame Press, 2007), 216.

15. Lisa Sharon Harper, *The Very Good Gospel: How Everything Wrong Can Be Made Right* (Colorado Springs, Colo.: WaterBrook, 2016), 40.

16. Andrew Schmutzer and Alice Mathews, "God Creates the World (Genesis 1:1–2:3)," Theology of Work Project, June 11, 2013, www.theologyofwork.org/old-testament/genesis-1-11 -and-work/god-creates-the-world-genesis-11-23.

17. J. K. Rowling, *Harry Potter and the Sorcerer's Stone* (New York: Scholastic, 1997), 50–51.

18. This is a riff off John Mark Comer's brilliance. John Mark Comer, *Garden City: Work, Rest, and the Art of Being Human* (Grand Rapids, Mich.: Zondervan, 2015), 61.

19. Richard J. Mouw, *When the Kings Come Marching In: Isaiah and the New Jerusalem,* rev. ed. (Grand Rapids, Mich.: Eerdmans, 2002), 11.

20. Timothy Keller with Katherine Leary Alsdorf, *Every Good En-*

deavor: Connecting Your Work to God's Work (New York: Penguin, 2016), 44.

21. Comer, *Garden City,* 54.

22. Barry Asmus and Wayne Grudem, "Property Rights Inherent in the Eighth Commandment Are Necessary for Human Flourishing," in *Business Ethics Today* (Center for Christian Business Ethics Today, 2011), 125, www.waynegrudem.com/wp -content/uploads/2012/03/Property-Rights-Inherent-in-the -Eighth-Commandment.pdf.

23. Phil Knight, *Shoe Dog: A Memoir by the Creator of Nike* (New York: Scribner, 2016), 353.

24. Quoted in Comer, *Garden City,* 41.

25. Richard L. Pratt, Jr., *Designed for Dignity: What God Has Made It Possible for You to Be,* 2nd ed. (Phillipsburg, N.J.: P&R, 2000), 7, emphasis added.

26. Martin Luther, *Luther's Works,* ed. Jaroslav Pelikan, vol. 14, *Selected Psalms III* (Saint Louis, Mo.: Concordia, 1958), 114.

27. N. T. Wright, *After You Believe: Why Christian Character Matters* (New York: HarperOne, 2010), 74.

28. Comer, *Garden City,* 63.

29. See footnote for Genesis 2:12, www.biblegateway.com/passage /?search=Genesis%202%3A12&version=NIV.

30. Makoto Fujimura, *Art and Faith: A Theology of Making* (New Haven, Conn.: Yale University Press, 2020), 80.

31. Wright, *After You Believe,* 76.

32. *Tangled,* directed by Nathan Greno and Byron Howard (Burbank, Calif.: Walt Disney Studios Motion Pictures, 2010), Disney+.

33. Tom Nelson, *Work Matters: Connecting Sunday Worship to Monday Work* (Wheaton, Ill.: Crossway, 2011), 60.

34. Andrew Schmutzer and Alice Mathews, "God Works to Create the World (Genesis 1:1–25)," Theology of Work Project, June 11, 2013, www.theologyofwork.org/old-testament/genesis-1 -11-and-work/god-creates-the-world-genesis-11-23/god-works -to-create-the-world-genesis-11-25.

35. James Davison Hunter, *To Change the World: The Irony, Tragedy, and Possibility of Christianity in the Late Modern World* (New York: Oxford University Press, 2010), 232.

36. Richter, *Epic of Eden,* 118.

37. Stuart Briscoe, *Choices for a Lifetime: Determining the Values That Will Shape Your Future* (Wheaton, Ill.: Tyndale, 1995), 142.

38. Asmus and Grudem, "Property Rights," 125.

39. *Office Space,* directed by Mike Judge (Los Angeles: Twentieth Century Fox, 1999), Hulu.

40. Kevin DeYoung and Greg Gilbert, *What Is the Mission of the Church? Making Sense of Social Justice, Shalom, and the Great Commission* (Wheaton, Ill.: Crossway, 2011), 210.

41. Hugh Whelchel, *How Then Should We Work? Rediscovering the Biblical Doctrine of Work* (McLean, Va.: Institute for Faith, Work & Economics, 2012), 33.

42. Isaac Watts, "Joy to the World," 1719, https://library.timeless truths.org/music/Joy_to_the_World.

43. "Was Jesus a Carpenter?," Got Questions, accessed January 24, 2023, www.gotquestions.org/was-Jesus-a-carpenter.html.

44. Klaus Issler, "Jesus's Career . . . Before His Ministry," Institute for Faith, Work & Economics, May 7, 2014, https://tifwe.org /jesus-career-before-his-ministry.

45. Issler, "Jesus's Career."

46. John Piper, "What Is the Kingdom of God?" *Ask Pastor John,* podcast, 10:26, September 8, 2017, www.desiringgod.org /interviews/what-is-the-kingdom-of-god; N. T. Wright, "N. T. Wright (Theologian)," interview by Jordan Raynor, *Mere Christians,* podcast, 53:07, June 16, 2020, https://podcast .jordanraynor.com/episodes/nt-wright-theologian.

47. Anthony A. Hoekema, *The Bible and the Future* (Grand Rapids, Mich.: Eerdmans, 1979), 53.

48. J.R.R. Tolkien, *The Lord of the Rings* (Boston: Houghton Mifflin Harcourt, 2014), 930.

49. Quoted in Fujimura, *Art and Faith,* 77.

50. Steven J. Lawson, *Heaven Help Us! Truths About Eternity That Will Help You Live Today* (Colorado Springs, Colo.: NavPress, 1995), 106.

51. "2041. Ergon," Bible Hub, accessed December 28, 2022, https://biblehub.com/greek/2041.htm.

52. Keller, *Ministries of Mercy*, 56.

53. N. T. Wright, *Surprised by Hope: Rethinking Heaven, the Resurrection, and the Mission of the Church* (New York: HarperOne, 2008), 204.

54. *The West Wing*, season 6, episode 7, "A Change Is Gonna Come," directed by Vincent Misiano, written by John Sacret Young and Josh Singer, aired December 1, 2004, on NBC.

55. Alicita Rodriguez, "Juneteenth History: Why Doesn't Everyone Know About Texas?," CU Denver News, June 8, 2021, https://news.ucdenver.edu/juneteenth-history-why-doesnt-everyone-know-about-texas.

56. "The Garden Tomb's Story," The Garden Tomb: Witness & Worship in Jerusalem, accessed December 28, 2022, https://gardentomb.com/about.

57. *Encyclopaedia Britannica*, s.v. "fish," last modified June 20, 2023, www.britannica.com/animal/fish.

58. Wright, *Surprised by Hope*, 210–11.

59. Lin-Manuel Miranda, "Waiting on a Miracle," *Encanto*, directed by Jared Bush and Byron Howard (Burbank, Calif.: Walt Disney Studios Motion Pictures, 2021), Disney+.

60. Lin-Manuel Miranda, "All of You," *Encanto*, directed by Jared Bush and Byron Howard (Burbank, Calif.: Walt Disney Studios Motion Pictures, 2021), Disney+.

61. Nancy Pearcey, *Total Truth: Liberating Christianity from Its Cultural Captivity* (Wheaton, Ill.: Crossway Books, 2004), 47.

62. Os Guinness, *Carpe Diem Redeemed: Seizing the Day, Discerning the Times* (Downers Grove, Ill.: IVP Books, 2019), 34.

63. Often attributed to J. Hudson Taylor, but no original source has been located.

64. Comer, *Garden City*, 107–8.

65. Darrell Cosden, *The Heavenly Good of Earthly Work* (Milton Keynes, U.K.: Paternoster, 2006), 110.

CHAPTER 2: HALF TRUTHS ABOUT HEAVEN

1. Joni Eareckson Tada, *Joni: An Unforgettable Story*, rev. ed. (Grand Rapids, Mich.: Zondervan Books, 2021), 70.
2. Tada, *Joni*, 44.
3. Tada, *Joni*, 88.
4. Tada, *Joni*, 89.
5. "Our Leadership," Joni & Friends, accessed December 28, 2022, www.joniandfriends.org/about/our-leadership.
6. Joni Eareckson Tada, "From Paralysis to Faith," interview by Larry King, *Larry King Live*, CNN, August 3, 2004, www.youtube.com/watch?v=P_ItOxB-JpM.
7. Tada, "From Paralysis to Faith," emphasis added.
8. *It's a Wonderful Life*, directed by Frank Capra (New York: RKO Radio Pictures, 1946), Amazon Prime.
9. Jason Byassee, "Surprised by N. T. Wright," *Christianity Today*, April 8, 2014, www.christianitytoday.com/ct/2014/april/surprised-by-n-t-wright.html.
10. N. T. Wright, *Surprised by Hope: Rethinking Heaven, the Resurrection, and the Mission of the Church* (New York: HarperOne, 2008), 197.
11. Lewis A. Drummond, *Spurgeon: Prince of Preachers* (Grand Rapids, Mich.: Kregel, 1992).
12. Often attributed to Charles Spurgeon, but no original source has been located.
13. Wright, *Surprised by Hope*, 201.
14. R. Paul Stevens, *The Other Six Days: Vocation, Work, and Ministry in Biblical Perspective* (Grand Rapids, Mich.: Eerdmans, 1999), 183; R. Paul Stevens, *Work Matters: Lessons from Scripture* (Grand Rapids, Mich.: Eerdmans, 2012), 6.
15. Sally Lloyd-Jones, "Treasure Hunt!," in *The Jesus Storybook Bible: Every Story Whispers His Name* (Grand Rapids, Mich.: Zonderkidz, 2007), 250.
16. Dallas Willard, "The Craftiness of Christ: The Wisdom of the

Hidden God," Dallas Willard, accessed June 10, 2023, https://dwillard.org/articles/craftiness-of-christ-uncut.

17. David Briones, "Already, Not Yet: How to Live in the Last Days," Desiring God, August 4, 2020, www.desiringgod.org/articles/already-not-yet.

18. Sandra L. Richter, *The Epic of Eden: A Christian Entry into the Old Testament* (Downers Grove, Ill.: IVP Academic, 2008), 219.

19. John Ortberg, *Eternity Is Now in Session: A Radical Rediscovery of What Jesus Really Taught About Salvation, Eternity, and Getting to the Good Place* (Carol Stream, Ill.: Tyndale Momentum, 2018), 33.

20. Rick Warren, *The Purpose Driven Life: What on Earth Am I Here For?*, rev. ed. (Grand Rapids, Mich.: Zondervan, 2012), 50–51.

21. Carrie Underwood, vocalist, "Temporary Home," by Luke Laird, Zac Maloy, and Carrie Underwood, track 8 on *Play On*, 2009, Arista Nashville.

22. Wright, *Surprised by Hope*, 41, emphasis added.

23. Mike Raiter, "Mansions in the Sky? Rethinking John 14:2," The Gospel Coalition, November 19, 2018, https://au.thegospelcoalition.org/article/mansions-sky-rethinking-john-142.

24. Wright, *Surprised by Hope*, 148.

25. Belinda Carlisle, vocalist, "Heaven Is a Place on Earth," by Rick Nowels and Ellen Shipley, track 1 on *Heaven on Earth*, 1987, MCA Records, emphasis added.

26. "Away in a Manger," *The Sunday School Hymnal* (New York: Reformed Church in America, 1899), no. 269, https://archive.org/details/sundayhym99efo/page/n257/mode/2up?view=theater.

27. John Mark Comer, *Garden City: Work, Rest, and the Art of Being Human* (Grand Rapids, Mich.: Zondervan, 2015), 239.

28. N. T. Wright, *The Early Christian Letters for Everyone: James, Peter, John, and Judah* (Louisville, Ky.: Westminster John Knox, 2011), 119.

29. John Eldredge, *All Things New: Heaven, Earth, and the Restoration of Everything You Love* (Nashville, Tenn.: Nelson Books, 2017), 28.

30. *Moana,* directed by John Musker and Ron Clements (Burbank, Calif.: Walt Disney Studios Motion Pictures, 2016), Disney+.

31. Skye Jethani, *Futureville: Discover Your Purpose for Today by Reimagining Tomorrow* (Nashville, Tenn.: Nelson Books, 2013), 30.

32. Jim Reeves, vocalist, "This World Is Not My Home," track 11 on *We Thank Thee,* 1962, RCA Victor.

33. Darrell Cosden, *The Heavenly Good of Earthly Work* (Milton Keynes, U.K.: Paternoster, 2006), 52.

34. Paul Marshall with Lela Gilbert, *Heaven Is Not My Home: Learning to Live in God's Creation* (Nashville, Tenn.: Word, 1998), 30.

35. Marshall, *Heaven,* 30.

36. Fleming Rutledge, *The Crucifixion: Understanding the Death of Jesus Christ* (Grand Rapids, Mich.: Eerdmans, 2015), 393.

37. Miroslav Volf, *Work in the Spirit: Toward a Theology of Work* (Eugene, Ore.: Wipf and Stock, 2001), 93.

38. Randy Alcorn, *Heaven* (Carol Stream, Ill.: Tyndale Momentum, 2004), 459.

39. N. T. Wright, *After You Believe: Why Christian Character Matters* (New York: HarperOne, 2010), 77.

40. Richard J. Mouw, *When the Kings Come Marching In: Isaiah and the New Jerusalem,* rev. ed. (Grand Rapids, Mich.: Eerdmans, 2002), 99.

41. Alcorn, *Heaven,* 95.

42. Mouw, *When the Kings Come,* 37.

43. Cosden, *Heavenly Good,* 75.

44. Cosden, *Heavenly Good,* 75.

45. Jodi Benson, vocalist, "Part of Your World," by Alan Menken and Howard Ashman, in *The Little Mermaid,* directed by John Musker and Ron Clements (Burbank, Calif.: Buena Vista Pictures, 1989), Disney+.

46. John Piper, *God Is the Gospel: Meditations on God's Love as the Gift of Himself* (Wheaton, Ill.: Crossway, 2005), 47.

47. Alcorn, *Heaven,* 135–36.

48. Cosden, *Heavenly Good,* 33.

49. Andy Crouch, *Culture Making: Recovering Our Creative Calling* (Downers Grove, Ill.: IVP Books, 2008), 171.

50. Eldredge, *All Things New,* 152.

51. Collin Hansen and Sarah Eekhoff Zylstra, *Gospelbound: Living with Resolute Hope in an Anxious Age* (Colorado Springs, Colo.: Multnomah, 2021), 26.

52. Isaac Asimov, quoted in Alcorn, *Heaven,* 409.

53. C. S. Lewis, *The Lion, the Witch and the Wardrobe* (London: HarperCollins Children's Books, 2015), 165.

54. Lewis, *Lion,* 165, emphasis added.

55. Vince Gill, "Go Rest High on That Mountain," track 11 on *When Love Finds You,* 1994, MCA Nashville.

56. "2041. Ergon," Bible Hub, accessed December 28, 2022, https://biblehub.com/greek/2041.htm.

57. Comer, *Garden City,* 260.

58. Karl Rahner, *Servants of the Lord* (New York: Herder and Herder, 1968), 152.

59. Jim Croce, "Time in a Bottle," track 8 on *You Don't Mess Around with Jim,* 1972, ABC Records.

60. Wilbur M. Smith, *The Biblical Doctrine of Heaven* (Chicago: Moody, 1968), 195.

61. *Chariots of Fire,* directed by Hugh Hudson (Burbank, Calif.: Warner Bros., 1981), Disney+.

62. James M. Campbell, *Heaven Opened* (New York: Revell, 1924), 123.

63. J. K. Rowling, *Harry Potter and the Sorcerer's Stone* (New York: Scholastic, 1997), 297.

64. N. T. Wright, *Paul for Everyone: 1 Corinthians* (Louisville, Ky.: Westminster John Knox, 2004), 225.

65. Wright, *Surprised by Hope,* 208.

66. Bruce Milne, *The Message of Heaven and Hell: Grace and Destiny* (Downers Grove, Ill.: InterVarsity, 2002), 257, emphasis added.

67. Wright, *Surprised by Hope,* 208.

68. Mark Batterson, *Win the Day: 7 Daily Habits to Help You Stress Less and Accomplish More* (Colorado Springs, Colo.: Multnomah, 2020), 108.

CHAPTER 3: HOW TO CONTRIBUTE TO GOD'S ETERNAL PLEASURE
EVEN IF YOU'RE NOT CHANGING THE WORLD

1. Chassie Anders, "Chassie Anders (Founder of Crown of Glory Beauty)," interview by Jordan Raynor, *Mere Christians,* podcast, 43:08, April 6, 2022, https://podcast.jordanraynor.com/episodes/chassie-anders-founder-of-crown-of-glory-beauty.

2. Chassie Anders, email message to author, December 10, 2021.

3. Anders, email message.

4. Anders, "Chassie Anders," *Mere Christians.*

5. Anders, email message.

6. Anders, email message.

7. Anders, "Chassie Anders," *Mere Christians.*

8. Anders, email message.

9. Anders, email message.

10. Chassie Anders, in discussion with author, September 2022.

11. Anders, email message.

12. Anders, email message.

13. Anders, email message.

14. Anders, email message.

15. Anders, email message.

16. Anders, email message.

17. Anders, in discussion.

18. Makoto Fujimura, *Art and Faith: A Theology of Making* (New Haven, Conn.: Yale University Press, 2020), 18.

19. Gustavo Gutiérrez, *On Job: God-Talk and the Suffering of the Innocent,* trans. Matthew J. O'Connell (Maryknoll, N.Y.: Orbis Books, 1987), 75.

20. Rick Warren, *The Purpose Driven Life: What on Earth Am I Here For?,* rev. ed. (Grand Rapids, Mich.: Zondervan, 2012), 71.

21. Warren, *Purpose Driven Life,* 66.

22. John Piper, "All of Life as Worship," Desiring God, November 30, 1997, www.desiringgod.org/messages/all-of-life-as-worship.

23. Patrick Lai, "Really! Work Is Worship," Business as Mission, July 4, 2016, https://businessasmission.com/really-work-is-worship.

24. John Coltrane, *A Love Supreme,* liner notes, December 9, 1964, http://albumlinernotes.com/A_Love_Supreme.html.

25. Timothy Keller with Katherine Leary Alsdorf, *Every Good Endeavor: Connecting Your Work to God's Work* (New York: Penguin, 2016), 249.

26. Keller, *Every Good Endeavor,* 249.

27. "2041. Ergon," Bible Hub, accessed December 28, 2022, https://biblehub.com/greek/2041.htm.

28. John Calvin, *Commentary on a Harmony of the Evangelists, Matthew, Mark, and Luke,* trans. William Pringle, vol. 2 (Edinburgh: Calvin Translation Society, 1845), 143.

29. R. Paul Stevens, *Work Matters: Lessons from Scripture* (Grand Rapids, Mich.: Eerdmans, 2012), 91.

30. Keller, *Every Good Endeavor,* 234.

31. Keller, *Every Good Endeavor,* 220.

32. Andrew Scott, *Scatter: Go Therefore and Take Your Job with You* (Chicago: Moody, 2016), 116.

33. Attributed to Howard Thurman in the introduction to Howard Thurman, *Democracy and the Soul of America,* ed. Peter Eisenstadt and Walter Earl Fluker (Maryknoll, N.Y.: Orbis Books, 2022), xi.

34. Eric Metaxas with Anne Morse, *Seven More Men: And the Secret of Their Greatness* (Grand Rapids, Mich.: Zondervan Books, 2020), 90.

35. Metaxas, *Seven More Men,* 109.

36. Quoted in Stan Klos, "George Washington Carver," George Washington Carver, December 20, 2012, www.georgewashingtoncarver.org.

37. Metaxas, *Seven More Men,* 100.

38. George Washington Carver, quoted in John Perry, *George Washington Carver* (Nashville, Tenn.: Thomas Nelson, 2011), 61.

39. Skye Jethani, *With: Reimagining the Way You Relate to God* (Nashville, Tenn.: Thomas Nelson, 2011), 87.

40. Fujimura, *Art and Faith,* 142.

41. Skye Jethani, *Futureville: Discover Your Purpose for Today by Reimagining Tomorrow* (Nashville, Tenn.: Nelson Books, 2013), 103.

42. Jethani, *With*, 86.

43. Jethani, *With*, 85.

44. Jethani, *With*, 87.

45. Robert Kurson, *Rocket Men: The Daring Odyssey of Apollo 8 and the Astronauts Who Made Man's First Journey to the Moon* (New York: Random House, 2018), 255.

46. Kurson, *Rocket Men*, 259.

47. Kurson, *Rocket Men*, 262.

48. *Moana,* directed by John Musker and Ron Clements (Burbank, Calif.: Walt Disney Studios Motion Pictures, 2016), Disney+.

49. Jenna Fortier, "Jenna Fortier (Student & Founder of PASTA)," interview by Jordan Raynor, *Mere Christians,* podcast, 37:26, September 30, 2020, https://podcast.jordanraynor.com/episodes/jenna-fortier-student-founder-of-pasta.

CHAPTER 4: HOW TO MAXIMIZE YOUR ETERNAL REWARDS AND ENSURE YOUR WORK *PHYSICALLY* LASTS INTO HEAVEN

1. Humphrey Carpenter, *J.R.R. Tolkien: A Biography* (London: HarperCollins, 2002), 260–61.

2. Carpenter, *Tolkien,* 260.

3. J.R.R. Tolkien, "Leaf by Niggle," in *Tree and Leaf* (London: HarperCollins, 2001), 94.

4. Tolkien, "Leaf by Niggle," 97.

5. Tolkien, "Leaf by Niggle," 102.

6. Tolkien, "Leaf by Niggle," 102.

7. Tolkien, "Leaf by Niggle," 117–18.

8. Tolkien, "Leaf by Niggle," 118.

9. Tolkien, "Leaf by Niggle," 109.

10. Tolkien, "Leaf by Niggle," 110.

11. Tom Shippey, *J.R.R. Tolkien: Author of the Century* (Boston: Houghton Mifflin, 2002), 276.

12. C. S. Lewis, "The Weight of Glory," in *The Weight of Glory and Other Addresses* (New York: HarperOne, 2001), 26.

13. Randy Alcorn, *Managing God's Money: A Biblical Guide* (Carol Stream, Ill.: Tyndale, 2011), 89, 104.

14. Joel Osteen, *Your Best Life Now: 7 Steps to Living at Your Full Potential* (New York: FaithWords, 2014).

15. J. C. Ryle, *Holiness: Its Nature, Hindrances, Difficulties, and Roots* (Peabody, Mass.: Hendrickson, 2007), 66.

16. John Eldredge, *All Things New: Heaven, Earth, and the Restoration of Everything You Love* (Nashville, Tenn.: Nelson Books, 2017), 114.

17. Aarti Sequeira, "Faith," Aarti, accessed January 3, 2023, https://aartisequeira.com.

18. Rick Warren, *The Purpose Driven Life: What on Earth Am I Here For?*, rev. ed. (Grand Rapids, Mich.: Zondervan, 2012), 71.

19. See Matthew 25:1–13 and Ephesians 5:25–27 as examples.

20. Randy Alcorn, *Heaven* (Carol Stream, Ill.: Tyndale Momentum, 2004), 200.

21. Joni Eareckson Tada, "From Paralysis to Faith," interview by Larry King, *Larry King Live,* CNN, August 3, 2004, www.youtube.com/watch?v=P_ItOxB-JpM.

22. Joni Eareckson Tada, "Joni Eareckson Tada (Painter)," interview by Jordan Raynor, *Mere Christians,* podcast, 28:54, June 15, 2022, https://podcast.jordanraynor.com/episodes/joni-eareckson-tada-author-of-the-awesome-super-fantastic-forever-party.

23. "What Is the Meaning of the Parable of the Ten Minas?," Got Questions, accessed January 3, 2023, www.gotquestions.org/parable-ten-minas.html.

24. Tada, "Joni Eareckson Tada," *Mere Christians.*

25. Arthur Miller, "Introduction to *Collected Plays,*" in *Death of a Salesman,* ed. Gerald Weales (New York: Penguin, 1996), 162.

26. According to the margin notes of the New American Standard Bible. See Alcorn, *Heaven,* 205.

27. N. T. Wright, *Surprised by Hope: Rethinking Heaven, the Resurrection, and the Mission of the Church* (New York: HarperOne, 2008), 193, 208.

28. Joel R. White, "Do Good Work (1 Corinthians 3:10–17)," Theology of Work Project, December 16, 2011, www.theology

ofwork.org/new-testament/1-corinthians/do-good-work-1
-cor-310-17.

29. Lesslie Newbigin, *Signs amid the Rubble: The Purposes of God in Human History,* ed. Geoffrey Wainwright (Grand Rapids, Mich.: Eerdmans, 2003), 47.

30. Skye Jethani, *Futureville: Discover Your Purpose for Today by Re-imagining Tomorrow* (Nashville, Tenn.: Nelson, 2013), 95.

31. Tolkien, "Leaf by Niggle," 97.

32. Tolkien, "Leaf by Niggle," 110.

33. Jim Elliot, "October 28, 1949," in *The Journals of Jim Elliot,* ed. Elisabeth Elliot (Grand Rapids, Mich.: Revell, 2002), 174.

CHAPTER 5: HOW TO SCRATCH OFF THE KINGDOM OF GOD AND YANK PIECES OF HEAVEN ONTO EARTH

1. Alister McGrath, *C. S. Lewis—A Life: Eccentric Genius, Reluctant Prophet* (Carol Stream, Ill.: Tyndale, 2013), 42.

2. McGrath, *Lewis,* 20, 42.

3. C. S. Lewis, *The Great Divorce: A Dream* (New York: HarperOne, 2001), 66.

4. C. S. Lewis, *Surprised by Joy: The Shape of My Early Life* (New York: Harcourt Brace Jovanovich, 1955), 179.

5. Terry Glaspey, *Not a Tame Lion: The Life, Teachings, and Legacy of C. S. Lewis* (Chicago: Moody, 2022), 38.

6. McGrath, *Lewis,* 42.

7. Lewis, *Surprised by Joy,* 179.

8. Terry Glaspey, *75 Masterpieces Every Christian Should Know: The Fascinating Stories Behind Great Works of Art, Literature, Music, and Film* (Chicago: Moody, 2021), 177.

9. Glaspey, *75 Masterpieces,* 177.

10. N. T. Wright, "Trevin Wax Interview with N. T. Wright on *Surprised by Hope,*" interview by Trevin Wax, The Gospel Coalition, April 24, 2008, www.thegospelcoalition.org/blogs/trevin-wax/trevin-wax-interview-with-nt-wright-on-surprised-by-hope.

11. N. T. Wright, *Surprised by Hope: Rethinking Heaven, the Resurrec-*

tion, and the Mission of the Church (New York: HarperOne, 2008), 111.

12. Randy Alcorn, *Heaven* (Carol Stream, Ill.: Tyndale Momentum, 2004), 48.

13. Wright, "Trevin Wax Interview."

14. Wright, *Surprised by Hope,* 259.

15. Glaspey, *75 Masterpieces,* 248.

16. Amy L. Sherman, *Kingdom Calling: Vocational Stewardship for the Common Good* (Downers Grove, Ill.: IVP Books, 2011), 18.

17. Bob Millsaps, "Our Children Are Watching—Four Keys On How To Build the Kindgom of God," June 18, 2017, https://folcc.org/our-children-are-watching-four-keys-on-how-to -build-the-kingdom-of-god.

18. Kevin DeYoung and Greg Gilbert, *What Is the Mission of the Church? Making Sense of Social Justice, Shalom, and the Great Commission* (Wheaton, Ill.: Crossway, 2011), 134.

19. Timothy Keller, *Ministries of Mercy: The Call of the Jericho Road,* 3rd ed. (Phillipsburg, N.J.: P&R, 2015), 31.

20. N. T. Wright, *Simply Christian: Why Christianity Makes Sense* (New York: HarperOne, 2006), 236.

21. DeYoung and Gilbert, *What Is the Mission,* 134.

22. Thanks to Dr. Amy Sherman for her help in building this list. Sherman, *Kingdom Calling,* 27–44.

23. Cornelius Plantinga, Jr., *Not the Way It's Supposed to Be: A Breviary of Sin* (Grand Rapids, Mich.: Eerdmans, 1996), 9–10.

24. John Mark Comer, *Garden City: Work, Rest, and the Art of Being Human* (Grand Rapids, Mich.: Zondervan, 2015), 61, emphasis added.

25. Hilaire Belloc, *Joan of Arc* (Boston: Little, Brown, 1930), 53–54.

26. Eric Metaxas, *Seven Men and Seven Women: And the Secret of Their Greatness* (Nashville, Tenn.: Nelson Books, 2016), 244.

27. Belloc, *Joan of Arc,* 54.

28. C. S. Lewis, *Miracles: A Preliminary Study* (New York: HarperOne, 2001), 244, 253.

29. Aaron Kuecker, "Confrontation over the Liberation of a Slave

Girl in Philippi (Acts 16:16–24)," Theology of Work Project, August 11, 2012, www.theologyofwork.org/new-testament/acts /a-clash-of-kingdoms-community-and-powerbrokers-acts-13 -19/the-community-of-the-spirit-confronts-the-brokers-of -power-acts-16-and-19/confrontation-over-the-liberation-of -a-slave-girl-in-philippi-acts-1616-24.

30. Os Guinness, *Carpe Diem Redeemed: Seizing the Day, Discerning the Times* (Downers Grove, Ill.: IVP Books, 2019), 27.

31. Jon C. Laansma, "Working Outside the Camp (Hebrews 13:11–25)," Theology of Work Project, May 4, 2012, www .theologyofwork.org/new-testament/hebrews/working-outside -the-camp-hebrews-1311-25.

32. Scott Johnson, "A Visit to Robben Island, the Brutal Prison That Held Mandela, Is Haunting and Inspiring," *Smithsonian,* May 2012, www.smithsonianmag.com/travel/robben-island-a -monument-to-courage-62697703.

33. Skye Jethani, *Futureville: Discover Your Purpose for Today by Re-imagining Tomorrow* (Nashville, Tenn.: Nelson Books, 2013), 80.

34. Nelson Mandela, *Long Walk to Freedom* (New York: Little, Brown, 2008), 489.

35. Mandela, *Long Walk to Freedom,* 489.

36. Jethani, *Futureville,* 81.

37. Wright, *Surprised by Hope,* 209.

38. Wright, *Surprised by Hope,* 209.

39. G. K. Chesterton, *The Everlasting Man* (San Francisco: Ignatius, 1993), 105.

40. Lewis, *The Great Divorce,* 83.

41. Jethani, *Futureville,* 112–13.

42. Ron Johnson, *Customer Service and the Imitation of Christ: A Spiritual Adventure in the Workplace* (self-pub., 2012), 8.

43. Johnson, *Customer Service,* 54.

44. Johnson, *Customer Service,* 54.

45. Johnson, *Customer Service,* 54.

46. Sho Baraka, *He Saw That It Was Good: Reimagining Your Creative Life to Repair a Broken World* (Colorado Springs, Colo.: Water-Brook, 2021), 30, 36.

47. James Davison Hunter, *To Change the World: The Irony, Tragedy, and Possibility of Christianity in the Late Modern World* (New York: Oxford University Press, 2010), 238–54.

48. Timothy Keller with Katherine Leary Alsdorf, *Every Good Endeavor: Connecting Your Work to God's Work* (New York: Penguin, 2016), 36.

49. Andy Crouch, *The Life We're Looking For: Reclaiming Relationship in a Technological World* (New York: Convergent Books, 2022), 126.

50. Dave Murray, quoted in Crouch, *Life,* 130.

51. Crouch, *Life,* 128–29.

52. Wright, *Surprised by Hope,* 200.

53. N. T. Wright, *Matthew for Everyone, Part 2: Chapters 16–28* (Louisville, Ky.: Westminster John Knox, 2004), 207.

54. William A. Ward, quoted in "Judge Each Day Not by the Harvest You Reap but by the Seeds You Plant," Quote Investigator, June 23, 2021, https://quoteinvestigator.com/2021/06/23/seeds.

CHAPTER 6: HOW TO MAKE DISCIPLES IN A POST-CHRISTIAN WORLD WITHOUT LEAVING TRACTS IN THE BREAK ROOM

1. Eric Metaxas, *Amazing Grace: William Wilberforce and the Heroic Campaign to End Slavery* (New York: HarperOne, 2007), 54.

2. Metaxas, *Amazing Grace,* 59.

3. William Wilberforce, quoted in Metaxas, *Amazing Grace,* 69.

4. Metaxas, *Amazing Grace,* 274–75; *Encyclopaedia Britannica,* s.v. "Slavery Abolition Act," last modified October 4, 2022, www.britannica.com/topic/Slavery-Abolition-Act.

5. Metaxas, *Amazing Grace,* xvii.

6. Metaxas, *Amazing Grace,* 167.

7. Metaxas, *Amazing Grace,* 234, emphasis added.

8. Metaxas, *Amazing Grace,* 234.

9. John Stott, *Christian Mission in the Modern World* (Downers Grove, Ill.: IVP Books, 2008), 43.

10. Kennon Vaughan, "Downline Discipleship, Marching Orders: Bringing Clarity to the Commission of Christ," *Downline Disci-*

pleship Curriculum (Memphis, Tenn.: Downline Ministries, 2022).

11. Bob Buford, *Halftime: Moving from Success to Significance,* rev. ed. (Grand Rapids, Mich.: Zondervan, 2015).

12. Timothy Keller, *How to Reach the West Again: Six Essential Elements of a Missionary Encounter* (New York: Redeemer City to City, 2020), 18.

13. Michael Green, *Evangelism in the Early Church,* rev. ed. (Grand Rapids, Mich.: Eerdmans, 2003), 243–45.

14. Monique Beals, "The Fastest Growing US Religious Affiliation? 'None,' Poll Says," The Hill, December 14, 2021, https://thehill.com/homenews/state-watch/585764-the-fastest-growing-us-religious-affiliation-none-poll-says.

15. Jillian Jenkins, email message to author, December 11, 2022.

16. Ron Johnson, "Ron Johnson (CEO of Enjoy)," interview by Jordan Raynor, *Mere Christians,* podcast, 39:49, June 22, 2022, https://podcast.jordanraynor.com/episodes/ron-johnson-ceo-of-enjoy.

17. Steve Martin, interview by Charlie Rose, *Charlie Rose,* December 12, 2007, www.youtube.com/watch?v=teAvv6jnuXY.

18. Andrew Scott, *Scatter: Go Therefore and Take Your Job with You* (Chicago: Moody, 2016), 177.

19. "Scatter Stories: How an HR Executive Reflects Jesus at Work," Scatter Global, December 15, 2021, www.scatterglobal.com/scatter-stories-how-an-hr-executive-reflects-jesus-at-work.

20. "Scatter Stories."

21. "Scatter Stories."

22. Michael Oh, "From Every Land to Every Land: The Internationalization of Missions—Its Potential and the Price," Desiring God 2011 National Conference, September 24, 2011, www.desiringgod.org/messages/from-every-land-to-every-land-the-internationalization-of-missions-its-potential-and-the-price.

23. Oh, "From Every Land."

24. Oh, "From Every Land."

25. Andrew Scott, "Andrew Scott (CEO of Operation Mobilization USA)," interview by Jordan Raynor, *Mere Christians,* podcast, 44:39, June 29, 2022, https://podcast.jordanraynor.com /episodes/andrew-scott-ceo-of-operation-mobilization-usa, emphasis added.

26. Credit goes to my pastor, Chris Basham, for this analogy.

27. Alfred Roberts, "The Inner Life" sermon notes, c. 1941, www .margaretthatcher.org/document/109901.

28. Alicia Grandey et al., "Free to Be You and Me: A Climate of Authenticity Alleviates Burnout from Emotional Labor," *Journal of Occupational Health Psychology* 17, no. 1 (2012): 1–14, https:// pubmed.ncbi.nlm.nih.gov/21875210.

29. Credit for these helpful terms goes to Matt Chandler. Matt Chandler, "The Breadth of the Gospel" (sermon, The Village Church, Flower Mound, Tex., September 7, 2021), https:// vimeo.com/599633559.

30. Metaxas, *Amazing Grace,* 167.

31. William Wilberforce, quoted in Reginald Coupland, *Wilberforce: A Narrative* (London: Oxford University Press, 1923), 236.

32. Coupland, *Wilberforce,* 237.

EPILOGUE: MAKE IT MATTER MORE

1. Craig Strydom, quoted in Mary Carole McCauley, "Ex-Baltimorean Went 'Searching for Sugar Man,'" *The Baltimore Sun,* August 27, 2012, www.baltimoresun.com/entertainment /bs-xpm-2012-08-27-bs-ae-sugarman-film-20120824-story .html.

2. *Searching for Sugar Man,* directed by Malik Bendjelloul (New York: Sony Pictures Classics, 2012), Amazon Prime.

3. *Searching for Sugar Man.*

4. *Searching for Sugar Man.*

5. *Searching for Sugar Man.*

6. *Searching for Sugar Man.*

7. *Searching for Sugar Man.*

ACKNOWLEDGMENTS

1. Sovereign Grace Music, "All I Have Is Christ," by Jordan Kauflin, track 2 on *30: Three Decades of Songs for the Church,* Integrity Music, 2014, www.youtube.com/watch?v=ug GucoYMmKg.

FREE RESOURCES FOR MERE CHRISTIANS

WORKBOOK

Want some help responding to the truths of this book? Download *The Sacred Response* workbook: a collection of more than twenty hyper-practical exercises to help you maximize the eternal impact of your work based on what you've learned in *The Sacredness of Secular Work*. Get the free workbook now at jordanraynor.com/response.

DEVOTIONALS

Every Monday, I publish a new devotional to help you more deeply connect the gospel to your work. It's called The Word Before Work, and it's available for you to read (via email), listen to (via podcast), or watch (via YouTube). Subscribe for free at jordanraynor.com/twbw.

PODCAST

Want to hear more stories from mere Christians like you and me who are responding to the sacredness of their seemingly secular work? Then the *Mere Christians* podcast is for you! I interview Christians from a wide variety of vocations to unpack how the gospel is shaping their work. Subscribe for free at jordanraynor.com/podcast.

FREE RESOURCES FOR PASTORS

I *love* the local church, which is why I want to equip you with tons of resources to help you help your flock see how their work matters for eternity. Specifically, I'm giving you . . .

- sermon outlines based on this book
- a list of popular terms shared from the pulpit that mere Christians find offensive (and which terms to use instead)
- best practices from other local churches for elevating the callings of congregants

Download all the above resources and more for free at jordanraynor.com/pastors.

JORDAN RAYNOR is a leading voice of the faith and work movement. Through his bestselling books (*The Creator in You, Redeeming Your Time, Master of One,* and *Called to Create*), the *Mere Christians* podcast, and his weekly devotionals, Jordan has helped millions of Christians in every country on earth connect the gospel to their work.

In addition to his writing, Jordan serves as the executive chairman of Threshold 360, a venture-backed tech start-up that Jordan previously ran, as CEO, following a string of successful ventures of his own.

Jordan has been selected as a Google Fellow twice and served in the White House under President George W. Bush. A sixth-generation Floridian, Jordan lives in Tampa with his wife and their three young daughters. The Raynors are proud members of the Church at Odessa.

Celebrate the Creator
in Your Child

This beautiful, playful, rhyming picture book shows children their role in God's creative work and celebrates God's call to create with him.

Also from bestselling author
JORDAN RAYNOR

Discover seven powerful time-management principles to become more purposeful, present, and productive in this biblical antidote to swamped to-do lists and hurried schedules.

A devotional featuring 260 readings, one for every workday of the year, to help you see how your work connects to God's work in the world.

Discover how to find and excel at the one thing you were made to do exceptionally well in service to God and others.